The MAN MANUAL

ALSO BY DR LINDA PAPADOPOULOS

Mirror Mirror: Dr Linda's Body Image Revolution

The MAN MANUAL

everything you've
ever wanted
to know about your man

DR LINDA
PAPADOPOULOS

HODDER
MOBIUS

First published in Great Britain in 2005 by Hodder and Stoughton
A division of Hodder Headline
This paperback edition published in 2006

A Mobius paperback

2

A CIP catalogue record for this title
is available from the British Library

ISBN 0 340 89829 1

Typeset in Sabon MT by
Palimpsest Book Production Limited,
Polmont, Stirlingshire

Printed and bound by
Mackays of Chatham Ltd, Chatham, Kent

Hodder Headline's policy is to use papers that are natural,
renewable and recyclable products and made from wood grown in
sustainable forests. The logging and manufacturing processes are expected
to conform to the environmental regulations of the country of origin.

Hodder and Stoughton Ltd
A division of Hodder Headline
338 Euston Road
London NW1 3BH

CONTENTS

Acknowledgements   ix

Welcome to *The Man Manual*   1

Part One The Beginning   39

Q. I like somebody, why isn't he making a move?   56

Q. How do I tell him I like him?   60

Q. Why doesn't he call when he says he's going to?   63

Q. Why does he want to rush into sex so quickly?   67

Q. Why does he get so touchy about me
    sleeping over?   71

Q. Why is he so jealous of my male friends?   75

Q. Why is he so competitive?   79

Q. Why does he want to sleep with me but
    not date me?   82

Q. I'm in love with my best friend. How do I
    tell him?   85

Q. Why is he such a flirt when he says he likes me?   89

Q. Why can't I get him to commit?   92

Q. My new boyfriend may be cooling off. Help!   96

Q. Why is he so cagey when I try to talk about
past relationships?   100

Q. He's still best friends with his ex. Should I be
bothered and what do I do if I am?   104

Q. How do I judge the pace at which the
relationship should be moving?   109

Q. He and my best friend hate each other. What
can I do?   112

Q. He's crowding me! How do I tell him I like him,
but I need my space?   115

Part Two The Middle   121

Q. How come his friends seem more important
than me?   137

Q. Why doesn't he share my passion for shopping?   142

Q. How come he finds it so difficult to be
romantic?   147

Q. Why is it taking forever for him to introduce me
to his parents?   151

Q. He was really into sex at the beginning, but he
isn't any more. Does he still find me sexy?   156

Q. Why does he need female friends when he
has me?   161

Q. We keep having the same arguments. How do
we stop going round in circles?   167

Q. Why does he put me down in front of his
friends?   171

Q. I think he still has feelings for his ex, what
should I do?   175

Q. We dated and now he just wants to be friends.
What can I do?   180

Q. Why have I started to feel trapped in this
relationship?   185

Q. I don't find him attractive anymore – why?   189

Part Three Happily ever after, or
happily ever after (but not with him . . .)   195

Q. How can I find out if he loves me without
scaring him away?   216

Q. Why does moving in together scare him so
much?   220

Q. Why does he have such a high tolerance for dirt? 226

Q. We've just moved in together. Why do we
fight about money?   230

Q. My partner's been unfaithful. Is this the
end of the relationship?   234

Q. My boyfriend is watching porn. What should
I do?   238

Q. Why has he become so withdrawn and moody?   243

Q. He says I'm smothering him and I feel we're never close enough. How can we resolve this? 247

Q. How do I tell him I want to take this relationship all the way to the altar? 251

Q. I love him but I just don't see us together forever. Should I end it? 255

This book is dedicated to my father Andreas and my husband Teddy, the two most important men in my life . . .

Thank you to Helen and Amy and everyone at Hodder for the great feedback and all the laughs throughout the whole writing process. To Jaine for being a great agent and a great friend, to Helen Brook for all the ridiculous anecdotes that arrived via my e-mail and gave me much needed breaks. To my wonderful family, especially you, Mom, for never complaining when I needed to make the time to write and for supporting me in each and every way. To my gorgeous little Jessica who makes my world a magical place and, especially, to the men in my life — my father Andreas and my husband Teddy, whose integrity, love and selflessness reconfirm my faith in men and humanity every day . . .

WELCOME TO
The MAN MANUAL

WHAT EVERY WOMAN NEEDS
TO KNOW . . .

What do Ikea flatpacks, microwaves, home hair-dying kits and mobile phones all have in common? They all come with instructions. They all come with handy little booklets explaining how to get the thing set up, how to use it and, if all goes the way of the pear, how to fix it. Orange-juice cartons come with instructions just in case you can't work out how to open them. Beautiful embroidered silk shrugs come with instructions to stop you hauling them in a sixty degree wash with your manky bed sheets. (As if.) You can't even buy a packet of crisps without being told where to dispose of the foil bag once you're done. Nearly every investment you make in life, from a mascara to your first car, will come with instructions. It makes us feel assured, safe and in control. We know that the best-before date is on the lid, but it's nice to have a little note on the side reminding us. We know that we should stop at the entrance to a dual carriageway, but it's good to have it scrawled on the road just in case. CD players, frozen pizzas, trainers, printers, in fact pretty much everything you can think of that a modern woman would need in her life, comes with instructions. But there's one exception. There's one asset that we invest in with absolutely no guidance and no handy manual. Men. Blindly, we put time and effort into a relationship, often to end up completely baffled by the output. It's a fact. Men do not come with a manual. Until now . . .

Because that's exactly what *The Man Manual* is (in case the name wasn't enough of a giveaway): a handy guide to accompany that man you just picked up at the store, or at a bar, or at work, or at the laundry . . . (What do you mean, 'that would never happen'? Don't you remember those Levi ads?!) *The Man Manual* is a instruction booklet to exactly what is going on in that mind of his, and what you can do to make him come round to your way of thinking . . . sorry, reach a *compromise*. Often the way we deal with men and the little dilemmas posed by their behaviour is completely wrong, because we don't understand the problem in the first place. *The Man Manual* will help give you some insight into why these things are happening, and then go on to help you deal with them in a practical way. It's divided into three parts, which correspond roughly to the stages of a relationship: the beginning, the middle and the happily ever after (or the end!). But before we get to that stage, it's important to understand a few of the basics about men. And before we do that, we need to think about ourselves. Because understanding relationships isn't just about understanding how the boys work. It's about working out the motivation behind our own behaviour. A good way to do this is to take a look at our own experience of relationships. So, [insert your name here], this is your (love)life!

Let's start at the beginning. Ever since we dressed Barbie

in her very best legwarmers and puffball skirt combo for her first date with Ken (come on, it was the eighties – even Barbie made fashion mistakes), women have appreciated the importance of a strong, healthy, romantic relationship. From the school playground, the rules of Kiss Chase encouraged an active, hungry pursuit of the perfect partner. OK, so perhaps it never materialised into the love of your life, but who can forget the moment of pride once you'd cornered gorgeous Jason from class 4C into a two-second snog in the sandpit.

And then there are the school discos. 'It doesn't matter if nobody asks you to be their date, darling,' assures your mum. 'It'll be fun to go with the girls.' No, Mum, it won't. It'll be about as much fun as getting dropped off in a van emblazoned with a 'Sad and Lonely' slogan, and wearing a dress sponsored by 'UglyandRepulsive.com'. Nothing compares to the desperate, sinking sensation as slowly every single one of your girlfriends is bashfully asked to the school social event of the year. You begin to regret unmercifully bullying that geek in maths, as even he manages to snag a date. You start to plan intricate methods of escaping the country – now, where does Dad keep the passports . . .

And then we hit the magical age of full-time jobs and full-time mortgage payments, or at least a hefty rent outcome. And suddenly summers are full of wedding after wedding, where of course we're put on the awkward leftover table with the children and that aunty with the bad breath. Or we find that 'nights out with the girls' increasingly become 'about the boys', involving argument-by-argument accounts of your friends' relationships. They try to muster up an interest in you, of course – 'So, how's work going then?' – but once you've exhausted the office gossip you can't help but feel that a summary of the outcome of your negotiations with a neighbouring firm is not quite what the girls were looking for. Dinner parties, birthday gatherings and the inevitable children's birthday parties become perfect opportunities to reinforce the feeling that not only have you been left firmly on the shelf but that everyone else has emptied the shelf, turned the lights off and left the room.

We put ourselves through virtual torture to remedy the situation, enduring silent dates, excruciating matchmaking introductions and painful chat-up lines, but why? When we finally find a man who makes it past the first date, whose monobrow and naff dress sense we can overlook, we spend as much time trying to figure out what he's thinking, why he's thinking it and then as much time again trying to pretend we haven't even thought about his thinking. We exhaust ourselves with creating the illusion of nonchalance, disinterest and aloofness only to check our voicemail sixty-five times a day and try to break into his email account.

Even once he's firmly in our grip, once he's become 'the other half', 'my partner', 'him indoors', we haven't got it all sorted. Because then there is a whole new set of issues to be handled, a whole new list of arguments to be argued. From his page-3 ex-girlfriend, whose breasts keep popping up all over the place, to the scars on your feet from treading on his Scalextric, which he refuses to put away properly like a good boy – the fun is just beginning. He hates your dad, you hate his mum. He hates the way you spend, you hate the way he dances. He thinks using your toothbrush is acceptable, you think using his to clean the toilet is a suitable punishment. He wants to turn the spare room into a games room, you want to paint it pale yellow because in your head it's the new nursery. You want to get engaged, he won't even engage in a conversation longer than five minutes (particularly when the rugby's on). It makes you wonder why we bother.

WHY WE DO IT: THE THEORIES

So why do we? Why do we put ourselves through this catalogue of disasters? Why on earth would we want to hurl ourselves into arguments in pubs, bed and selected furniture stores? What makes us strive for relationships when they're so hard?

The Mating Game

Thousands of years ago, being an independent woman didn't really cut it. The fact is that hanging out by yourself, appreciating some 'me time', was all very well until somebody or something decided you were that evening's dinner. Once a great grizzly or a prehistoric diner decided you'd go brilliantly with a side of onion rings, no amount of throwing your hands up at Destiny's Child would save your bacon. 'Safety in numbers' had an entirely different meaning. Also, our predecessors figured pretty early on that the best way to survive as an enduring species was to reproduce. The more the merrier, and you weren't much good as a baby-maker if you were too busy sat on a rock criticising Caveman Colin's excess nasal hair, or fretting over whether or not he's been displaying 'commitment issues'. No, the point was to get together and make babies. Pairing up was essential to keep the species going. It wasn't a fun way to spend a Saturday evening or a dating game. It was a matter of survival, like sleeping, breathing and eating.

Evolutionary psychologists say that this primeval need to procreate is the real reason that we long for that special someone. Essentially, our purpose on this planet is to reproduce, and they say that this underlines our desperate attempts to find the perfect relationship. So, when we think we're looking for someone to put a name to that 'and guest' space on all our invitations, or just someone to choose lampshades with in Habitat, really we're scouting out a prime mating partner.

According to evolutionary psychologists, the other reason we strive to be half of a couple, in addition to mating, is just because deep down we still possess the basic need to be around others. To an extent that no other species demonstrates, humans are social beings who need to be around one another. It's one of the reasons that solitary confinement is considered a pretty tough punishment. OK, when in a busy supermarket on a Saturday afternoon, surrounded by your fellow human beings shouting, screaming and swearing, it might seem like a preferable choice, but in the long run humans crave company. It's why we talk about having somebody to grow old with. It's why so many love songs lament loneliness and being alone. Humans need to be with other humans. And this need, coupled with another basic need, to reproduce, is the reason that evolutionary psychologists claim that we long for relationships.

The (Peer) Pressure's On

Ever felt like you're surrounded by love, romance and sickly-sweet couples? Perhaps you've sat down to enjoy a loaded BLT at lunchtime to find yourself greeted by a sexy, skinny couple writhing around all over each other in the name of a new Gucci perfume ad? Or perhaps you've left a family gathering, battered into a state of mental breakdown after a barrage of questions that begin 'How's the love life?', 'Any wedding bells yet?' or 'So, is there a special someone yet?' According to social psychologists, these seemingly daily occurrences are the type of triggers that persuade us that we should be striving for a relationship.

These psychologists say that the world around us convinces us that we are only valid if we are part of a couple. And anybody who's ever been single has felt that pressure. It might be because of the ticket-seller at the cinema. It's a Thursday night. You can't persuade anyone to come and see the new Brad Pitt blockbuster so you decide that, after all, the point of the cinema is to watch the film and why do you need someone to go with anyway? You play your rubbish Power Ballads Sung By Men with Bad Mullets compilation CD on the way to the cinema, and you sing along with Michael Bolton et al because there's no one to tell you not to. Empowered, liberated and emboldened you stroll up to the ticket booth. 'Just one ticket please!' you demand, head held high. Then it begins, the fifteen-year-old serving you first of all asks you to repeat yourself. So you do. Then, still convinced you would never be so stupid and sad to go and perve on Brad on your own, he begins to check behind you for the signs of a man, or at least a couple of girlfriends. Nope. Suddenly, that single self-confidence begins to drain away. And there's no sympathy from the smug couples surrounding you, who are also baffled by your odd predicament.

And it doesn't get any easier once you make it into the film. Because nobody can name a romantic comedy where the end result isn't a blissfully happy couple. Even action films usually try to incorporate a little ill-fated love between a gangster's moll and a guy from the wrong side of town. In movieland, happiness equals being with someone, whether that manifests itself as a big romantic wedding scene or a life-threatening gesture of lifelong devotion. No wonder that every time you walk out of a cinema you feel like declaring your undying love for someone, even if it's the damn car park attendant.

Social psychologists would also use the advertising industry as further evidence for their theory that it is the outside world that conditions us into thinking we need to be in a relationship. Strangely, the cynical bunch don't quite believe that a shower gel can turn you into a love god who will be worshipped, or that a certain chocolate bar can lead to cosy nights in with a male model by a log fire. The fact is that most adverts operate along a set narrative: if you buy this product, you will be more attractive to the opposite sex, and therefore you will have your pick of the bunch, and therefore you will find the perfect partner, and therefore you will become complete. Lucky you. And all for the price of a lip gloss.

And those who don't buy into the race for a man? Sad. Lonely. Bitter. To say the least, of course. Just as the media portrays the happy glow of coupling in an established and predictable way, it also portrays single girls in a rather tried-and-tested manner. You can be scatty, snivelling and searching, à la Bridget Jones, or the alternative is feisty and fast – think Jordan, who is consistently portrayed as a rather cheap, sad example of what will happen if you just can't settle down. If you're not prepared to slot neatly into the couple box, then, ladies, these are your options. If you're going to go it alone, then you're going to have to develop an affinity for neurotic diary writing, or PVC knickers and furry dancer's boots.

Social psychologists say that friends can also be part of the machine that persuades us that we need to be in a relationship. When everyone you socialise with appears to be attached to someone else it can be hard. It takes guts to be the only single person at a dinner party or to arrive at a wedding reception alone. And it can be a soul-destroying moment when you realise that your friends actually feel sorry for you. Sure they tell you that they admire your single lifestyle, but every now and then you can tell that they'd never swap their comfy sofa on a Saturday night for your raucous nights out on the town.

So, in short, social psychology argues that rather than being a basic need or urge, in fact being in a relationship is something that we are conditioned to think we need. The world around us convinces us that we need to date and eventually become a couple with somebody, anybody.

It's All About Sex . . .

The biological perspective has a far more straightforward explanation for our desire to be part of a couple. According to the biologists, our need to be a 'him and her' is not about pressure from our parents or about bullying from society. It's not even about longing for companionship. No, they say it really is as basic as a need for sex. As humans we all possess a sex drive to some extent and in some form. Our attempts to be with somebody else are simply an attempt to fulfil that sex drive. And in a crude sense, aside from hanging around dirty nightclubs with dirty men, having a serious relationship is the surest way of guaranteeing that physical contact. Psychologists say that the pursuit of that kind of pleasure is part of a healthy human attitude. However, men and women can view it very differently.

Research has shown that when pursuing a relationship and, more specifically, sex, women are often craving the emotional connection that it can bring. So, the minute just after, when he looks so helplessly into your eyes before he falls asleep, or the gentle stroking of your hair in the morning – that's what the girls are after. Conversely, with the boys it's far more about the physical contact. Hair stroking and deep, powerful speeches about everlasting love and your undying commitment to him (admittedly performed in your underwear) are probably rather lost on him immediately after the deed itself.

Most women have experienced this fundamental difference in the way men see sex first-hand. Some of us have felt the rather disappointing realisation that, actually, that amazing, bonding, soaring connection you just made in the bedroom didn't mean quite the same thing to him. And you know it didn't mean quite the same thing to him because while you lay awake reflecting on it for hours and secretly wondering if it was just the tonic you needed to move your relationship forward, he's fast asleep, snoring at a volume that is threatening to cause a seismic earth tremor. Lovely. And more than that, the experts have found much the same thing. The makers of Viagra have completely abandoned their attempts to prove that the male impotence drug can have the same effect on women. Because, you see, we're just more complicated. Scientists have found that in men arousal always leads to desire, so libido can be improved by improving a man's ability to get an erection. Makes sense, right? Yes, but in women the link between arousal and desire is far more complicated. We can be physically aroused yet, mentally, more psychological factors come into play. Physiologically, our body reacts to sex in a far more complicated fashion, and psychologically it does too. This could explain why fewer than half as many women are likely to have extramarital sex as men. We simply find it harder to divide sex and our emotions.

So, the biological perspective asserts that we look for relationships because we need to communicate physically with others. The manner in which we seek relationships and the attitude with which we view them can be greatly affected by external influences. For example, if your family has taught you that sex is wrong and dirty, then you may well have problems feeling that you have the right to an active and enthusiastic sex life. Equally, if your man has been brought up in a family that does not show physical affection, then he might find it hard to bridge the gap between that non-contact and sex.

BASIC BIOLOGY: THE MALE

An understanding of the male body explains a few psychological features of the male mind. So, ladies, if you would be so kind as to turn to page one of your textbooks, let the lesson begin. Let's start at the top.

The Brain

The male brain is entirely different from the female brain. For example, take multitasking. We can all remember a time when we've cooked the evening meal, plucked our eyebrows and put rollers in, while selecting an outfit. Meanwhile, he can't answer a question as simple as 'What time is it?' because he is 'concentrating' – on washing a tomato! Baffling. Likewise, we manage to type a letter to the bank while speaking to his mother on the telephone. You could put him in an empty room with your mother, with no other distractions, and he'd still struggle to concentrate on exactly what she's saying. And there might actually be a genetic reason for this, although you probably shouldn't let him in on this nugget of information – he'll be citing it for years to come as an excuse.

Research has shown that men have a less efficient version of the gene that controls how easily we can switch our attention. And as well as genetic evidence there is also a school of thought that suggests that his inability to multitask springs from ancient history, years before the phrase had even been invented. When primeval females watched the children, organised the community and threw another pterodactyl leg on the fire for hubby when he came home from hunting, they probably didn't describe it as multitasking. But that is exactly what they were doing. Meanwhile, her mate's objectives were far more straightforward. Find, chase, kill, carry, eat. This history, although it doesn't bear much resemblance to modern life (well, apart from the bit where he comes home and wants to eat), could have a big impact on the way men still function today.

The Heart

Let's move down a little now, so on to the heart. Now, for all their macho bravado and boy talk, everybody can spot a man who is genuinely in love. All right, you might have to wrestle with him to make him actually say those three little words, but deep down you know he's smitten. There's a common misconception that men just aren't as emotional as women. After all, he doesn't cry at pictures of starved puppies, he didn't look even remotely moved when Scott and Charlene finally made it down the aisle in *Neighbours*, and getting him to talk about his feelings is like asking a footballer to talk about fine art. However, it's not that men don't feel the same emotions as us. It's just that they feel less comfortable expressing them. So perhaps he had a little snivel in his room about Kylie and Jason – OK, so he probably didn't. But when it comes to more serious matters he feels emotion just as strongly as you do. Evolutionary psychologists argue that the difference in communication is because women, historically, have always had more opportunity and, incidentally, time to talk about their feelings. (Chitter chatter about your deepest insecurities doesn't sit well with a race to see who can spear the biggest boar.) This has developed into a culture where children are told 'big boys don't cry', and, perhaps consequently, suicide rates are highest amongst young men. Women have been socialised into expressing their feelings far more readily than men. So, when you feel that he hasn't told you he loves you enough times in one day, rather than blaming yourself or him, it makes more sense to just remember and accept these basic links between emotion and gender. You'll know how he feels because he'll find other ways of showing you.

The Arms

Now, let's move down and out a little to the arms. Pay careful attention to these because hundreds of years ago those arms were used to protect, to hunt and to guard. Now, they're more likely to cook a fried-egg sandwich (for himself) or hold a video game controller for hours and hours on end. And now, of course, you're more than capable of providing for yourself, thank you very much. Traditionally, men have been providers and protectors: guarding the family, who are raised by the mother. A pattern was established whereby people were assigned roles depending solely on their gender. If you were a man, you were handed a spear and told to go find food, no matter how fast it runs. If you were a woman, you were used as a breeding ground for nine months before beginning the task of rearing your children. And this pattern continued until relatively recently.

The suffrage movement was one of the first initiatives to challenge these historic stereotypes. The feminist movement of the 1960s took things a little further, boasting groups such as the National Organisation for Women. And finally, in the early part of the twenty-first century, women are playing on a field that is more level than ever before. Women and men are free to go to the same places, do the same jobs and earn the same amount of money. So where does this leave the boys? Every part of his history tells him he should be providing and protecting. But how can he provide for you if you're earning twice as much as he does? And how can he protect you when you don't even want him to open doors for you? This shift in gender-assigned roles can cause conflict because we are socialised into believing that certain situations are desirable, even normal. This puts unrealistic pressure on you and him. You feel guilty about your success because your mother thinks your man should earn more than you, and he feels like he isn't fulfilling his duty to you because he always felt that he would provide for the woman in his life. Dealing with and challenging these norms can be an essential part of any relationship.

The Stomach

Now down to the tummy. He probably prefers you to call it his 'stomach' because it sounds more muscly, so we'll go with that for argument's sake. This area symbolises the relationship men have with food and their bodies. The chances are that whether he is the proud owner of a tight six-pack or a rather more rounded keg he's probably fairly happy with his body. While you squint, squirm and make mock-vomit noises in front of the mirror, he strolls past, has a quick glance, pats his hairy, wobbly little gut and grins, before polishing off the takeaway you deprived yourself of earlier. Men really do have a much healthier relationship with their bodies than women. Again, this is largely due to the way we have been socialised. For years, women were valued solely for the way they looked, and we were subjected to some pretty unrealistic role models.

Men have always been valued and assessed predominantly for their achievements and their successes, so the way they look has consequently been less important. Admittedly, recent years have placed more emphasis on male vanity, and the boys have had a few media-marketed role models of their own, take the Chippendales or Peter Andre's nineties six-pack. But in general, looks have always been less important for men, so they don't feel the same pressure as women to look perfect.

Body image can be important within a relationship if there are massive differences in how you each feel about your bodies. He might not understand why you insist on making love with the lights off, or why you burst into tears every time he makes a joke about your 'cuddly tummy'. (When will they understand that we do not, repeat, do not like words like 'wobbly', 'cuddly' or 'squidgy'?) Also, the way we feel about how we look is inextricably linked to our general self esteem, and this can have a big impact on how we conduct ourselves within relationships.

The Crown Jewels

Next, on to that boxer area. And no, you can't just scoot back a few pages and reread the 'Brain' section. We can look back to our ancestors again to explain a little bit about how his 'other brain' works. Ancient man cottoned on to the fact that the survival of the species was heavily dependent on reproduction. Therefore, sowing seeds all over the place was the way forward. Putting all your eggs in one basket or seeds in one field was not the most efficient way of ensuring you produced numerous offspring. Therefore, random sex with random women kept the species going without the hassles of what evolutionary psychologists call 'pair bonding'. If you zoom forward a few thousand years, getting every girl that they sleep with pregnant might sound like a young man's worst nightmare. In fact, for most of them it is. But the basic urge to spread the seed is still there, even if the desired result is different. It is just an ingrown feature, like the urge to provide or the urge to spend every Sunday down the pub with his friends. But don't let that be his excuse for flirting with every female within ten metres or ogling page 3 with an enthusiasm that you're sure is unhealthy. If he points to *FHM* and cites genetic make-up as his justification for a rather, ahem, *crowded* lovelife, then suggest that the species has evolved, and if he disagrees then perhaps he would like to revisit some other ancient caveman rituals. Like wearing animal print. (And we're not talking Gucci here . . .) And catching his own dinner. (It's slightly more testing than popping to Waitrose or waiting for you to rustle something up.) And administering foot rubs every night. (OK, so we made that one up, but try it, you never know . . .)

However, this could conflict with the way you see sex. Men typically attach less emotional importance to sex and view it in a far more functional manner. This can be great for getting a sense of reality and taking the pressure off both of you. But if he sees it as just sex when to you it's something more, then it can be disastrous for your self-esteem. To you, sleeping with him for the first time might be a symbol that you trust him and are willing to let him into your life a little more. And that's great, but not if to him it's just another notch on his seriously eroded bedpost.

The Feet

And finally, we move on to the feet. Big, smelly, hairy and the best metaphor there is for his commitment issues. Because those feet can make the difference between him digging his heels in and staying put, or doing a runner and sprinting away from any sign of commitment. It is common for men to have problems with commitment. We've all encountered that man who won't hold hands in public. Or the man who won't call you his girlfriend even though you've been going out for three years. Or the man who doesn't think snogging girls in nightclubs is cheating, as long as you don't find out about it. It's easy to think that men just want to have their cake and then eat it, but there are actually some deeper reasons for his fear of commitment.

Commitment means different things to men and women. Bachelorhood has long been glamorised and dressed up to be sexy, stylish and the epitome of a cool, single lifestyle. A long-term girlfriend who you refer to as 'snookums' doesn't really fit into this picture. Conversely, being a single young female, or worse a single aging female, has always had an entirely different stigma attached to it. Bridget Jones has always been seen as a little bit of a laughing stock in her desperate attempts to snag a man. The boys got James Bond, we got snivelling, diary-obsessed Bridget. For women, commitment is about gaining something; for men, committing can often mean losing something. And this can cause major disagreements about where your relationship is heading.

So there you have Diagram A: The Male. And we've pointed out a few of his weird and wonderful features.

The next step is figuring out exactly how you tackle some of the issues that arise just from him being a man and you being a woman.

MEN AND WOMEN ARE DIFFERENT

That may sound like a no-brainer, but it's crucial. If the psychologists behind the evolutionary perspective, the biological perspective and the social perspective assert that we need relationships so badly, then why are they so hard? Surely it should be simple? It is in the movies – boy meets girl, they fall in love, they have beautiful children and a beautiful house, and live happily ever after.

Well, the problem is that men are not women and women are not men. Of course, you might call this a rather simplistic view and you'd probably be verging on totally correct. But the premise is this: so many of the problems men and women face in relationships are simply due to the fact that we look at life so differently. We communicate differently, we understand differently, we behave differently, we dress differently. (OK, I know you're thinking about the Beckhams, but there's an exception to every rule.) In short we deal with relationships in ways that aren't even similar, and that is why so often we can't make sense of each other.

Right from the very start it's clear that there are a number of massive differences between men and women. And we're not talking in terms of equipment here. Because back in the maternity ward, before you'd even had a chance to suss out exactly what was going on in that department (largely due to your preoccupation with bawling at that man in the white coat who kept slapping you, and the woman who insisted on wiping off all the goo that, frankly, you'd become quite fond of), it's decided for you. Before Mum and Dad have even told you you're a Christina or a Christopher, a Brooklyn or a Britney, you're wrapped in something that clears the matter up once and for all. You're either a blue blanket or a pink blanket, and there are no two ways about it. And although every parent will insist that their offspring is the world's most beautiful child, the truth is that (and whisper it in case any new mothers hear you) all newborn babies look the same. It's tough to distinguish one sleeping, crying, guzzling bald head from another. So that blanket is fundamentally important in establishing at least one clue to your individuality. Later on, that blue blanket will translate to a blue nursery, then a set of trucks, then an Action Man, then a BMX, then a souped-up boy-racer-mobile with chrome alloys and sixty-five exhausts. Meanwhile, a pink blanket will inevitably lead to a fetching shade of strawberry sorbet in the nursery, pretty party frocks, dolls with 'real-life' tears, skipping ropes, perhaps a pony, and a lifetime of handbags and shoes. Being born a female marks us as different from men from the word go.

Despite this, one of the biggest mistakes women make in building relationship is thinking their man is a woman. Of course, we know they're not (despite his increasing interest in fake tan and waxing), but we still expect them to behave like one. We expect – no – we want him to deal with things our way. So, when we say, 'I'll call you,' we have a list of considerations in mind. Do I sound too keen? Too controlling? Should I specify when I'll call? Should I give him my number too? How long should I wait before

I make the phone call? What if we have nothing to say to each other? What if he doesn't answer? Should I leave a voicemail? If I do, what should I say? What if he doesn't call me back?

Now, a man has a very different set of considerations. He says, 'I'll call you' as he drops you off, then he gets distracted by a smug guy in the brand-new BMW, completely forgets the conversation and heads home for a microwave dinner. Meanwhile, you're still analysing those three words. In fact, days later, particularly if he hasn't called, you're still analysing, although as the days go by the words sound more and more empty as you repeat them in your head. Eventually, you drive yourself into a state of insanity where you can't actually bear to hear the words 'I'll', 'call' and 'you'. In any order. Which makes everyday conversation a little difficult. Now, of course, the absence of his immediate phone call doesn't necessarily mean that he isn't interested. In fact, calling you is probably on his list of things to do. Unfortunately for you, it was added after 'clean room', 'iron work shirts' and 'call Mum'. Blame his absent-mindedness, blame his lack of organisation, but don't turn the delay into clear evidence of his indifference to you. Yes, if it were the other way round, perhaps *you* would have called exactly one and a half days after your first date. But he isn't you, and he doesn't think like you. And this isn't necessarily a bad thing.

'So, men and women are different?' you ask. 'How on earth did you spot this astonishing revelation? Perhaps the physical differences or maybe a few other clues – dress sense, taste in music, standards of hygiene, levels of football knowledge, interest in celebrity gossip, number of shoes owned and ability to do sixty-five things at once?

Oh, and comprehension of the rules of golf?' It might sound blindingly obvious. Of course men and women are different. But it is our emotional make-up that can cause conflict in relationships, rather than your failure to appreciate his yearly membership to the Metallica fan club. Let's take a look at the big things that set the boys apart from the girls.

HOW TO TALK ABOUT A PROBLEM

Women frequently talk about how they want their man to be more sensitive or more 'emotionally available'. In truth this often makes as much sense as wishing he had breasts and a cupboard full of Manolos. Or when he makes a mistake, women falsely assume that he has put as much energy into it as she'll put into discussing it with her girlfriends and crying herself to sleep. For example, if a man cheats, women look for reasons all over the place. Does he feel that I don't show him enough affection? Is he trying to get rid of me? Does he still love me? The profound implications of the infidelity are often completely lost on the man, who attributes far less symbolic relevance to it. That doesn't mean that men are too stupid to register that infidelity is wrong or likely to hurt you. It means that because it is not a relationship-changing issue for him, perhaps he can't see why it is to you. So, he drunkenly snogged that girl from the office? It isn't a big deal to him, after all it has no bearing on his feelings for you, so why should it be to you? Also, men are far more solution-focused than women. So, if a mishap like this does occur, while the woman is dwelling on it and running and rerunning it over in her head, the man has probably moved forward, attempting to get the relationship back on track. This can be wrongly interpreted as a lack of interest or unwillingness to deal with the problem, when in fact he *is* dealing with the problem, just in a typically masculine way.

Evolution is often cited as an explanation for the difference in the emotional make-up of men and women. It's been suggested that the responsibility of minding children while the men were off hunting fine-tuned women's sensitivity as they became more alert to threats to their little ones. This developed into a far higher level of perception than men possess. So that same instinct that previously could have prevented your offspring from becoming somebody's dinner, can now help you spot a woman who's eyeing up your man, or work out when he's fibbing about how many pints he's had. Another theory argues that because most of the important decisions were made by the men, for the women worry became their work. So while he was deciding whether veal or pork was on the menu tonight, you would have been discussing the smaller matters in life such as Cave-lady Colette's new haircut. And finally, there's also the idea that because there were so many places where women simply were not allowed, they gained a greater grasp of their emotional territory. While the men were free to explore, women were often cooped up in the home, so they took greater control and made greater explorations of their emotions.

Traditional roles can also affect not just how emotional we are but the things we get emotional about. Research has shown that women are far more likely to get emotional about relationships, births and reunions. This is because, historically, the woman was the caretaker, who was concerned with the more social side of running a family. Conversely, men, the stereotyped providers, are more likely to be affected by world events, illnesses and achievements. This will come as no surprise to the women who have nursed a ridiculously over-acting man with a cold. (Never before have you appreciated his superb acting talents until you hear those Oscar-winning snivels coming from the sofa.) Likewise, we get angry about different things. Women are far more likely to be angry about a perceived violation to the relationship, while men become angriest about threats to their autonomy. So while him taking a girl's number in a bar might send you into a plate-hurling rage, he's far more likely to explode once you tell him that if he leaves the house after dark again it's over.

And on a smaller scale, women often deal with lesser discrepancies in a similarly epic style. We've all done it. You come in from work exhausted, feeling like you're not being (a) taken seriously, (b) paid enough and (c) invited to the hen night that everyone else in your office appears to be heading off to. You kick off your shoes, collapse on the sofa and go to pick up the TV listings. Then you spot it. Glaring at you from the kitchen work top. Almost laughing at you. No – cackling. He's done it again, after all you said. Not only can you spot the dirty plate from his dinner but he's managed to use six saucepans, a sieve, the scales, every one of those hanging kitchen tools, two mugs and, bizarrely, a rolling pin. You know he used all of this stuff because it's all sitting there covered in the remnants of tonight's culinary delight: pasta in a sauce. You feel your blood boil – and not because he's been a little uneconomical with pots and pans (although how he managed to use the entire contents of the Habitat kitchen section for fresh pasta and a jar of sauce, you'll actually never understand) – but because to you, this means so much more. He has ignored your polite request that he kindly leave the kitchen in the state that he would like to find it. He has gone to bed and left you to deal with the messy predicament. But more than that, he has disrespected you. He has spitefully lashed back at your reasonable request. Your relationship dynamics have completely shifted. He's lost interest and doesn't care about your happiness any more.

Now, of course, again, he is completely in the dark about this slightly manic train of thought, but it's far too late for him to catch up with you. You're streets ahead, building scenario by scenario as you clank the soapy plates around in a manner specifically intended to wake him up, so that you'll get the opportunity to blow him to kingdom come with your anger. To him, he's just forgotten. That's it. He ate dinner, began watching the rugby, then started to fall asleep so he dragged himself to bed. No blatant breaches of your relationship rules. No lack of respect. No intentional insults. He just forgot. And he'll do it tomorrow anyway. Of course he won't understand your anger, in the same way as you can't understand his indifference.

The key to dealing with this, and where *The Man Manual* comes in really handy, is teaching yourself to just accept that men feel so differently about situations to you. The answer is to take a step back and try and appreciate that he isn't viewing the situation through your eyes. So, for example, you might have just realised that you are truly, madly, deeply in love with your best male friend. And you think he feels the same way. You're desperate to make a grand gesture of love but feel he should make the first move. So you wait and wait and wait. Eventually, because he hasn't hired a helicopter to fly a banner above your garden or commissioned Stevie Wonder to write you a love song, you decide he clearly isn't in love with you. So you give up and move on. The poor guy may well be in love with you, but just terrified by the situation, completely unaware of the best way to express his feelings.

Men are generally less emotionally literate than women. Researchers have stated that although emotion knows no gender, and men and women experience the same emotions, women tend to experience these emotions with a greater intensity. In addition to this, women are far more comfortable talking about their feelings than men. In general, women are more emotionally evolved. Women have been nattering about their feelings, their emotions, their moods, their desires for as long as they could talk. It's different for men, talking about feelings is often far harder. Research shows that mothers talk to their daughters more about emotions. For example, a mother might say to her daughter, while reading a story, 'How do you think the tortoise feels about the fact that the hare has beaten him? Does he look sad? Is he upset?' On the other hand, despite the development of political correctness and the 'equal' society we live in today, boys are often encouraged to deny feelings of vulnerability and to demonstrate a stiff-upper-lip mentality. If we are socialised into behaving a certain way, it's very hard to suddenly become more expressive and open. In a survey, 80 per cent of women said that they regularly cry. The same amount of men said that they didn't.

This difference in the way we express emotion makes

for a whole load of frustration, because when a problem arises, while you want to set up a summit with a chairman, minute-taker and witnesses to 'talk about things', he wants to hide in the corner and wait for the storm to blow over. You think it's because he doesn't care and can't be bothered to rectify the problem. But realistically, this misconception is a result of you judging his reactions based on what you know about yourself, not what you know about him. So, you know that if there is a situation that you don't analyse, assess and scrutinise that's probably because you don't consider it important enough. And that's saying something considering the things you deem worthy of the aforementioned analysis – like last night's *EastEnders*, the new Dior range and your manager's new haircut. So, when he says he doesn't want to talk, you immediately see the situation through your eyes and assume he feels the problem is unimportant. Cue misunderstandings, emotional blackmail and a bewildered boyfriend.

That's the reason why, when the tables are turned and he feels unhappy, he may well deal with the situation by, well, not dealing with it. Well, at least that's how you see it. You look at the brooding, quiet stranger who has moved into your flat and assume he is bottling up his troubles. In actual fact he is dealing with them in his own way. But, because sitting down and talking about the issues really helps you, you can't understand why it won't help him. The trick is to appreciate that he probably endures your talking, so you should learn to accept his brooding. Men tend to be less confrontational about issues, so his idea of fun is not an hour and a half discussion about exactly why he sighed when you asked him to pick up your mother from the airport or why he's been quiet for a whole morning.

This avoidance of confrontation also manifests itself long before we reach the arguments-over-the-dinner-table stage. Often, when a woman decides that her latest love interest isn't quite 'the one', she'll agonise over exactly how to tell him. She'll prepare a number of tactful, but relatively truthful, dumping excuses then spend hours working out ways to present these excuses in a cushioned, sensitive way. She might even prepare a few future recommendations and provide a reference for potential girl-friends. In fact, she'll probably find that she commits more to the dumping than she ever did to the relationship. The location, method and timing of the break-up will be planned impeccably over long coffee breaks with the girls. Then, of course, after the deed has been done the massive de-brief will begin.

Now, let's look at the average man's escape route when he decides that the new lady isn't the right lady. It's fairly seamless, at least to the unsuspecting woman. You've prob-ably been there. You think it's going OK. You've moved past the awkward first-date stage. Then one day he says, 'I'll give you a call,' just like he always does, so you don't really notice it. Until he doesn't call. You call the phone company demanding that they check your line because it's clearly broken. You go to the doctors to check your hearing because there's always the chance that perhaps you didn't hear the phone ring. And finally, after demanding that a Taiwan factory send you a new mobile phone because the six replacements you've had clearly were not accepting and registering incoming calls, you resign yourself to the fact that he just isn't going to call. If he wasn't interested, then why didn't he just say? Well, because in this case we are again expecting men to behave like a woman. You see it as wimping out, he sees the 'I'll call you' line as a deft, foolproof manoeuvre out of a relationship that isn't quite worth sacrificing bachelorhood for just yet. Why spend hours justifying his choice to you when he's not interested in spending any more time with you anyway? Of course, as a woman, this doesn't make sense to you. You want to have it out with him (so that explains your drunk phone calls at three in the morning!) and you want him to reason a decent argument. He just wants to get away from the situation.

HOW TO DEAL WITH A PROBLEM

Have you ever wondered why you sit with an Ikea flat-pack for days, throwing screwdrivers at the wall in fits of frustration and cursing everything Swedish, yet he can bang a lovely mahogany wardrobe together in less than five minutes? Or why he always seems so confused and stunned by your mid-argument recollection of that time six months ago when he said you were looking a little more cuddly? Men are far more solution-focused than women. While we are dwelling in the past, your man is far more likely to be looking for a way to 'fix' the problem. When there is a problem, women want to talk, discuss, share. Men want a troubleshooting guide. Which is where they're a step behind the ladies. Because that's exactly what *The Man Manual* is: a troubleshooting guide. Identify the problem by examining the symptoms, and go straight to the appropriate course of action. It really couldn't be easier.

When difficulties arise in relationships, or even before

you get that far, men and women often clash because their approaches to the problems are so different. Men are practical beings. They like nice straightforward solutions, preferably aided by tools and a bit of elbow grease. So, when he feels that there are problems within the relationship, he approaches it in an entirely different way to a woman. For a start, his focus will immediately be on the solution rather than the problem. Now, this technique works brilliantly in the office, or even on the football pitch on a Sunday morning, but not quite so well in a relationship. Because the two methods clash. Women's problem-solving techniques are far more complex than men's. They tend to focus more on the actual situation without visualising a solution in the same way that men do. As we've mentioned before, they ascribe far more symbolic importance to aspects that men simply miss.

So, here's an example. You sit your man down and say you need to talk to him. He's instantly a little defensive, as he can tell from your tone that this isn't about what he wants for dinner or what he needs to wear to Ben and Jill's wedding on Saturday. He sits, nervously eyeing you up and down. Then you begin, a little tearfully. You don't feel like he's there for you any more, you tell him. He seems distant and uninterested, you don't do enough things together and you feel unappreciated and a little unloved.

Now, ideally you'd like him to want to chat about exactly why you feel this way, perhaps ask for some examples of when he has made you feel like this and then try to understand your concerns. In reality, his answer is, 'OK, I won't go to the pub tonight then. I'll stay in.' Of course, then you begin a long explanation about the difference between physical presence and emotional availability, at which point you've completely lost him because you're beginning to sound rather like a woman's magazine.

The situation here causes problems for two reasons. Firstly, (we talked about emotional literacy earlier) men just aren't as clued-up on understanding a lot of the emotional issues that women talk about so freely. So this could provide a little background to explain why, when you're telling him that you feel like he's distant and uninterested, he doesn't really understand where you're coming from, and if he does understand the chances are that he'll be less able to put it into the language that you do. Even from before birth women display signs that they're going to be the real talkers: between eight to twenty weeks' gestation, female foetuses move their mouths far more often and for longer periods than male foetuses. So really, we've had a head start on the guys.

The second problem is that he has reached immediately for what he sees as a solution, missing much of the meaning of what you are saying. He hears, 'You're not there for me.' He refers to the instructions, turns to the trouble-shooting page and deduces that the correct response and plan of action is to sacrifice a night in the pub so that he can be 'there for you'. And, of course, this isn't what you mean, but the core differences between men and women dictate that these type of misunderstandings are commonplace in relationships. You tell him that he doesn't pay you enough attention, he assumes a bouquet of cheap carnations from the petrol station will do the trick. You tell him that it makes you feel uncomfortable when you see him flirting with other women, he promises to only do it behind your back. As far as he's concerned you're dwelling far too much on the problem, while he's looking for a way to fix it. Equally, you feel that he isn't taking the time to understand exactly why you feel the way you do, instead he's just looking for an easy solution.

HANG ON IN THERE!

Relationships are an essential part of life. We learn so much more and feel so much more when we're doing it with someone else. And in fact, as much as some of them appear to be dragged into relationships kicking and screaming, men need relationships even more than women. Figures from the Office of National Statistics show that married men actually live longer than single men, men who lived alone were at an increased risk of dying from a variety of illnesses. With divorced men, the figures showed that if they remarried their survival chances were increased. So, next time he's moaning about going shopping for the thirtieth time for an engagement ring because you still can't decide, just remind him that it really is in his own interests to toe the line!

The Man Manual won't teach you how to manipulate your boyfriend into seeing things like a woman (as tempting as that sounds), but it will help you to understand why he doesn't and it will teach you the best way to deal with that. Just make sure he doesn't catch you sneakily referring to it under the dinner table, as he silently pushes his food around the plate, mulling over some conundrum in his head. He'll only see it as cheating. Which it probably is!

HOW TO USE THIS BOOK

The problems we encounter when dealing with the male of the species vary greatly depending on what stage of the proceedings we're at. So, you probably won't be having issues about the spark going out of your relationship in the first week (if you are then start seeing big warning triangles). Likewise, you're unlikely to be arguing about him failing to commit ten years in (again, if you are this should be a rather big clue that all is not 100 per cent right). So *The Man Manual* is divided into three parts.

The first part will deal with the beginning. The 'honeymoon period'. Apparently. Because as much as the first few weeks or months are supposed to be full of hearts and flowers, the reality is often different. This is when we are attempting to find the right man, tell him he's the right man and work out how that complicated mind of his works. This stage can be fun, exciting and thrilling, but it can also be frustrating and confusing. Part One deals with a few problems that many women face in those tenuous first weeks. Think of it as a essential guide to the new man in your life.

The second part will deal with that stage that occurs once you've found your feet a little. You know he's into you and you know that you're into him, so to an extent some of the uncertainty has gone. However, this next stage brings a host of new problems. Why does he insist on seeing his old school friends so much? Why have I started to feel a little trapped? The answers to these types of questions are the ones that will help your relationship move seamlessly from the beginning stage to a more concrete phase. Well, almost.

And finally, we come to the real feet-under-the-rug stage. You're settled, he's settled and you're both in this for the long haul. You've stopped looking for other men, worrying about your bikini line and wearing matching underwear. You might have made the moving-in-together decision. So you thought you knew his ins and outs? Wait until you've seen his idea of 'clean' and heard his shower-wailing every morning for six months. Maintaining and cultivating a serious relationship requires at least as much effort as finding one in the first place. So the final part deals with a few of the hurdles you and your man might come up against once you've made a firm commitment to one another. ·

Each section is based on real letters I've received from women dealing with men. Of course, over time, several recurring questions arise. So, while only one woman hated the colour of her husband's car and wondered whether this was serious grounds for divorce, hundreds wondered if it was normal for him to be friends with his ex, or agonised over whether or not their man was cheating on them. These are the types of questions that are addressed. If you've ever wondered 'Why does he do this?' or 'Why can't he just do that', then your question has probably been pondered by a hundred other women. So you'll probably find the answers between these pages.

Each question is dealt with in the same way. First there will be a psychological explanation of what is going on. So you'll begin to understand why, sometimes, 'I'll call you' means 'I won't call you' and 'I love you' might just mean 'I'd love to have sex with you.' You'll begin to understand why he sulks and you cry. And you'll see why the C-word (Commitment – whisper it!) is such a big deal to him. The bit you've been waiting for will follow: the answer. How you deal with the problem. Using this information, guidance will be offered on how to address this situation so that you both feel happy with the outcome. And finally, think back to your textbooks at school. Remember how if you really couldn't squeeze in time for your homework (amidst the six hours you spent chatting to your newest love interest on your parents' phone bill and painting your nails the latest shade of pink) there was always a little cheat. Remember at the end of each chapter there was always a 'Key Points' section that would give you a quick, snappy summary of the preceding reams of tedious information? Genius. Well, each question answered by *The Man Manual* also has a few quick tips that take you straight to the crux of the action you should take. So just in case that hottie from work is steadily approaching your desk and you haven't quite memorised the best way to ask him out, you've still got time to have a quick peek. Just try and ensure you have an excuse ready when he notices you furiously flicking and asks what you're reading. Or it could get embarrassing.

None of the answers involves tears, tantrums or illegal brainwashing. They do, however, feature frank, realistic advice. So, as an example, the answer to 'How can I get him to commit?' will not be to get him drunk and coerce him into a Britney-style waltz up the aisle in Vegas. Sometimes the answers won't be what you want to hear. But they will be the best way to understand the male psyche and then deal with the man in your life. And once you've dealt with your one, you can be the envy of all your friends as you advise Oprah-style on their man worries. Use the book as it was intended – as a fun, honest and informative manual to the male mind. It's certainly more entertaining than the one you got with the dishwasher . . .

Part One

THE BEGINNING

THE HONEYMOON STAGE, HOPEFULLY . . .

Some people love the beginning of relationships. They thrive on the excitement of 'will he call or won't he call?'. They find the insecurity, the uncertainty, completely irresistible. Other people hate it, longing for a level playing field where everybody knows exactly where they stand. They're driven completely insane by the confusion and etiquette of today's dating games.

Everyone has experienced that beginning stage. It's where he can say, 'I'll call' without risking an ear-bashing if he doesn't, because a major feature of this stage is the pretence that you really aren't interested. So, if he doesn't call, while you may have broken three mobile phones in fits of rage that he hasn't kept his casually-pledged promise, you will, of course, greet his eventual communication and brief apology for the delay with, 'Oh, did you say you'd call? I totally forgot anyway, so don't worry about it! I've just been so busy'.

The beginning stage is where you're not quite sure whether or not you should be informing your parents of the new man's existence. Of course, your friends all know that your office crush has developed into a fledgling 'thing', but telling the old people is an entirely different ball game. Because you see romantic dinner dates, and they see church weddings and pushchairs. And, of course, there's always the fear of jinxing the whole damn thing. You can guarantee that the minute you feel a little too comfortable, a little content and secure (well secure enough to feature new man in your answers to 'So, how's the love life?'), the phone calls will stop, the flowers will die and any evidence of your fantastic new union will slowly fade away.

Much of the beginning stage involves sussing out what the other person is thinking. Just sorting out where they are, where you are and how the two meet. Sounds easy. Cue weeks of missed signals, imagined signals and misinterpreted signals. If only men appreciated the analysis and dissecting that goes on every time they make a phone call or send an email, they'd run a mile and lead a reclusive life miles away from any of those terrifying women.

The fact is the beginning of relationships are battlefields of misunderstanding, confusion and insecurity. Yes, it can also be a time of excitement, anticipation and that funny butterfly feeling in your tummy, but for many the experience is less than enjoyable. There are a couple of steps you can take to make sure that you go into the situation with the best possible attitude.

COMPLETE YOURSELF

Think about why you want to kick off the relationship with Mr Whoever. If it's because you just want somebody to stay in with on the cold winter nights, then perhaps you need to reassess your motives. We've talked about the pressures that play a part in convincing us that we are only valid once we come as half of a pair. Deeply-established ideas of gender-role assignment can make people believe that every ying needs a yang, that every good man needs a good woman and vice versa. Biology dictates that at least physically, men and women do need each other to procreate. And everybody has felt the pressure of a 'plus one' invite.

One of the most dangerous beliefs to carry into a new relationship, though, is the idea that you need to find your other half. People search the planet in the belief that one day they'll bump into the perfect person who will make them complete. *Jerry McGuire* has got a lot to answer for. Sure, Tom Cruise's dramatic speech to Renée Zellweger may have tugged a few heartstrings as he declared, 'You complete me', but it also helped reinforce a few relationship myths.

Asking somebody to complete you is a pretty tall order and, in practise, probably impossible. So you might have felt unhappy within yourself for years. You might feel that the perfect man will answer all your questions and right all your wrongs. Surely all those things you dislike about yourself, like your job, your temper and your thighs, he can change or at least change the way you feel about them? Surely he'll make you stronger, smarter and sexier? Of course you'll walk down the street and instantly be respected and admired because you're with Him? No. No. No. And sadly, no. You can't bring a half-cooked you to the relationship and expect him to take over the kitchen and finish you off beautifully.

Instead, bring a complete, assured, strong person to the table. You need to work on your self-esteem by yourself, because at the end of the day it's not really anybody else's responsibility. And because you can bring so much more to a new relationship when you're confident with who you are and what you can give to somebody else. Nobody else can improve the way you truly feel about yourself. And if you've placed your self-esteem and self-belief entirely in the hands of one person, what will you do if the relationship ends? Don't look to someone else to complete you. If you don't feel complete, then work on completing yourself. Because nobody else can do it for you.

True happiness in a relationship comes from knowing that you would survive without that person, but you have made a choice to be with them because it makes life more fun. So your relationship should feel like a choice and not like a necessity. If you view your man like a life-support machine, then something needs to change. Because if you feel like your world would end and you would possibly cease to breathe should he leave, then you put yourself in a highly vulnerable position. And you put him under a lot of pressure. It's a lot more enjoyable for him if he knows that you're there because you've chosen to be. He wants to know that you are a strong, desirable woman who could be just as happy on her own as you are with someone but you have chosen to be with him. Wow, what a confidence boost. So, before you go searching for someone to become the other half, make sure you are whole yourself. Then anything else is just an added bonus.

SET BOUNDARIES

Part of figuring out who you are before you set off in search of love's great dream, is knowing what you want and don't want from another person. Right from the start, be clear about why you are ready to embark on something with this person, and what you expect if you do step it up a little. Part of this is about being clear on who you are exactly. If you are a compulsive shopper who needs to spend every Saturday shoe-worshipping in Russell and Bromley, then fine. If you are obsessed with doing laundry three times a week, then so be it. On a more serious level, if you detest swearing and find it disrespectful, then that is part of who you are. If you won't tolerate your boyfriend staying out every night of the week, then that is a core part of your personality. If you insist that you switch your mobile phone off when you're having lunch with the girls, even if that makes him a little nervous, then fine. And if you know that you don't feel comfortable sleeping with someone until you have known them at least six months, then who is anybody to tell you that you're wrong? Define yourself and get to know yourself. Enter into a relationship with yourself in the same way as you would enter into a relationship with anybody else: find out what you like and what you need, and then work out ways to meet these requirements.

Setting clear boundaries means that you are more likely to get what you want from the relationship. When you begin negotiations at work, you lay out your expectations and what you want to gain from the job. When you establish a relationship with your employer, you enter into a clear deal where you tell them your expectations and your needs and he informs you of his. Equally, when we stay in a hotel, or buy clothes, or even order a baguette, we are clear on what we will and will not tolerate. Remember this when entering into a romantic relationship.

Part of knowing who you are is knowing what makes you happy and unhappy. You should have a clear definition of yourself before you enter into the relationship, or there is a danger that the relationship could start to define you. You might begin to accept things that perhaps don't fit your ideal, because they appear to be happening as part and parcel of the relationship. So suddenly you find that you're one of those couples who stay in and watch football highlights on a Saturday night. You used to be a girl that demanded to spend those evenings in a nice bar or a cosy restaurant with your man, but this makes him happier so this is what you've become. And you don't want him to leave so you accept it. And suddenly not only have your boundaries shifted, they've upped sticks and vanished.

Be clear about what you need from a relationship, and you are far less likely to find yourself settling for less. Because when you know what you want, you know when something is what you don't want. It cuts out nights spent on pointless dates with men who, ultimately, will never be right for you. It minimises weeks arguing over things that, if you'd thought about in the beginning, you would never have to deal with now, because you would have realised these things would never change and represented a massive breach of the rules you'd set yourself about what you would accept from a man.

Setting clear boundaries in the beginning stages also means that there are no nasty surprises for anyone later on. After all, what's the point in convincing that channel-hopping businessman that you are willing to relocate to wherever his firm decides to do business if realistically you are not prepared to ever leave the village you grew up in? Where's the sense in pretending you are cool with the new man traipsing into your room at three o'clock every morning and singing rugby songs before vomiting into your waste paper basket when you've got work the next morning if, in three months time, you're going to explode and scream that it's always driven you mad? Equally, you need to let the man know what he can expect from you. So make it clear if you need to spend at least three nights a week in your own bed alone. Warn him that you are an outrageous flirt but that it doesn't mean anything. Alert him to the fact that you'll probably be shy in front of his friends at first because that's just the way you are. That way he knows what to expect from you, just as you know what to expect from him. It means that both of you can be free to relax in the knowledge that you won't be letting anyone down by simply being yourself.

REMEMBER: A LITTLE COMPROMISE CAN BE A GOOD THING . . .

Having said all this, part of adapting to life with somebody else is accepting that things do change. Suddenly you roll over to be greeted by a big snoring lump in the middle of the night. You'll probably have to stop accepting dates from other men. And it's not OK to drunkenly snog men on stag dos anymore. Just because your principles and requirements shouldn't have to change when you begin a relationship, it doesn't mean that your lifestyle won't. When we accept somebody else into our agenda, inevitably we have to make changes. And this means knowing which of your boundaries to stick to and which you can afford to be a little lenient with. Having true conviction in your beliefs means allowing them to be challenged and deciding whether there is room for any leeway. So you might conclude that your rule to abstain from sex until you've been with him at least four months is one that you need to stick to, but you can relax the military style rules you'd established on eating in the living room. Perhaps you still want to spend half the week in your flat, but on at least some of those nights he's allowed to join you, as long as he turns down the volume on the TV.

While you should never abandon your boundaries, you can adapt them. You have to accept that some of your boundaries may clash with some of his, and if he's really worth holding on to then a little compromise may well come in handy. Perhaps you can extend him a little more freedom on the weekends if he promises to phone you before he's had too much to drink. Maybe you can try getting home from work a little earlier so he doesn't feel that he is becoming second-best. Instinctively, you know whether a decision to change feels like a sacrifice or a compromise, you know whether you feel assertive or weak when making it – so pick wisely.

Another thing to remember when you embark on a new relationship is that everybody has a little history that will affect the way they view situations and the boundaries they create for themselves. Human beings aren't like those etch-a-sketch toys that can be shaken after each use to reveal a blank canvas. We're more like plasticene, every experience we go through leaves a little mark, and then it's impossible to go back into the exact shape we were before. We need these experiences because they help us to learn and grow. They teach us about life and about love. But they can be a nightmare when it comes to opening yourself up to a new person and being flexible with your expectations. Because they can also be a little scarring. For example, if every man you've ever been with has cheated on you, the fact that you can be too suspicious and jealous with your new man is understandable. Or if your boyfriend is still carrying a little resentment and hurt from a painful break-up, this may affect the extent to which he feels comfortable relaxing with you. Screaming, crying and demanding he talk to you more won't help. A little understanding probably will.

The fact is that each time we commit ourselves to somebody for a certain amount of time, they leave a mark on our lives. And, inevitably, they affect the girlfriend you will be in the future. It's important to realise this for two reasons. Firstly, it helps you to understand why your partner is behaving a certain way – if you know that his last girlfriend slept with his best friend, you can do more to appreciate his fears that he will be hurt again. And if he flies off the handle when you say you're going on a big night out with the girls, you can understand his strength of feeling a little better. The second reason is that it helps you understand your own behaviour. If your last partner was abusive in any way, being aware of the impact of that on you will help you to understand why you shy away from confrontation with your new boyfriend, even though all he wants is for you to feel comfortable enough to disagree with him. It helps you to see things with a little perspective. You can take a step back and think, 'Am I reacting this way because this is the action the situation requires, or am I reacting this way because insecurities from a previous relationship are coming back to me?'

Demons from past loves are hard to banish. In fact,

they're nearly impossible to completely kill off. But with the right person, in the right relationship, you can view them with the awareness that will help you move on.

GAME-PLAYING AND HOW TO AVOID IT

Power games can act like a lethal shot in the arm of new love. And we've all played them. 'I'm not ringing him first!' we declare after the date from heaven. 'I don't want him to think I like him,' we assert about the man whose surname our signature fits so well with because we've spent approximately five weeks doodling it. We act coy. We act uninterested. In fact, sometimes we act as though we are harbouring a deep dislike for the man in question.

We've all done it – noticed the potential love of our life wander into the pub, and instinctively begun to flirt outrageously with whoever's next to us. Poor Bob – Mum and Dad's friend from down the road – doesn't know what's hit him. One minute you're barely concealing your boredom as he compares your dad's new hatchback to his jazzy new estate number, the next you're all over him. He's never seen you squeeze out a cleavage by squidging your arms to your chest before. He's never noticed your fillings, because you've never thrown your head back so hard that it nearly falls off at one of his jokes before. And he's certainly never heard you call him 'tiger' before. *Strange youth of today*, he puzzles.

That'll get him, you assure yourself. Lovegod will spy you having copious amounts of fun with another man, he'll be overcome with jealousy and march over to tear you away, demanding that the greying man in the flat cap and sheepskin jacket backs off, so that the two of you can run off into the sunset together. The whole episode will leave Bob from down the road a little confused, but at least you'll have snagged aforementioned Lovegod. Apart from, isn't that him that you can see leaving the pub, just walking through the door now? Yes. Oh well, you console yourself, another chance to pretend I'm completely un-interested will arise soon enough.

It's no surprise that the beginning of relationships is so fraught with confusion when everybody's so unclear about what they want from each other. The problem is not being bad at games, the problem is being good at games. You might feel that you've played it perfectly, that you've acted suitably nonchalant, that you've given him no hint that you like him. The main drawback here is that he has no hint that you like him! Playing a little hard to get can some-times work wonders, but try not to play so many games that you play yourself out of the game.

Forget the rules and old wives' tales that tell you that he should be making all the first moves. In an ideal world, of course, we'd all be swept off our feet by knights on white horses, who spend every waking minute booking exciting dates in breathtaking locations with confidence and aplomb. But the real world is not like the ideal world. More often it'll be a case of Kevin from reception plucking up the guts to ask you for a coffee in the staff canteen. So take a little bit of initiative yourself, help him along – without fear that you'll appear too keen. And if you have a great date and you really enjoy yourself, then don't worry that picking up the phone and telling him will make you appear like an obsessive stalker. It'll probably be music to his ears. Extend him the honesty that you expect in return. And if you must play games, then play fair. If your flirting and slight cajoling has finally persuaded him to invite you out for dinner, don't sit around for hours waiting until a suitable amount of time has lapsed so that you don't appear to be interested or anything. Accept gracefully. Keep the games to a minimum.

TRY NOT TO GET INTO FAST FORWARD MODE

It's a dangerous moment when your brain begins to work at double speed. Or even triple speed. You drop your bag in the supermarket, swear a little, then bend down to pick up your make-up, manky tissues, tampons and all the other rubbish that lurks in there. As you do, the tall, athletic man next to you bends down to help. Initially embarrassed by the afore-mentioned tissues and tampons, you smile at him. He smiles back. And suddenly your brain has pressed its own fast forward button. You see him helping you home with the shopping, then making you dinner, then charming your parents, then proposing, then telling you he wants six kids, then buying a country manor house with you, and then you see him growing old and distinguished in a Robert Redford-type way. All before you've even said 'thank you'. OK, so it may not materialise into anything other than small talk over your need to purchase a new handbag, but the accelerated daydreams can play havoc.

Getting caught up in the excitement and thrill of a new love is easy. Many of us find ourselves choosing kids' names before we know his last name, or telling friends that this one's 'the one'. So what if we've only been on two dates? So what if he's a little older (OK, three times your age)? It's love and you know it. Well, at first. And then the cracks begin to show and you suddenly begin to regret integrating your CD collection alphabetically with his. The deposit on that four-bedroom house doesn't seem like such a wise investment. And you begin to wish that the tattoo across your shoulder blades had been a little more ambiguous than 'Lucy loves Craig forever and ever'.

Die-hard romantics will argue that when it comes to love, common sense just doesn't enter the equation. They'll say that you should be swept away. That you should go with your heart and not with your head. But a little restraint can be your best tool in negotiating a new relationship. Don't make any rash decisions. Don't decide that friends are an unnecessary luxury now you have found the man that you're sure you will spend the rest of your life with. Keep a sense of perspective. Pace the feelings you are experiencing. After all, if this one truly is 'the one' then he'll still be around tomorrow, the next day and years to come after that. So what's the rush? You leave yourself in a rather vulnerable position if you offer your heart and soul from the starting gun. Hold back a little and remember how easy it is to get swept away by your feelings.

WE'VE ONLY JUST BEGUN . . .

New relationships are nothing to be scared of. They shouldn't evoke fear and dread, rather they should be exciting and thrilling. But there are a few things that you can do to make sure that amongst all the butterflies and lovehearts, you remain true to yourself and how you expect to be treated. That doesn't mean that you can't scream with excitement after putting the phone down when he first asks you for dinner. It doesn't mean that you can't start dreaming about how beautiful his babies will be. It just means that you keep reminding yourself what you want and who you are. The advantages of this are two-fold, so listen carefully. Firstly, you're far more likely to end up achieving the relationship you long for if you are clear about exactly what you want. Secondly, men are far more attracted to women who are strong and confident, and who are clear about their boundaries. It's far sexier to be 'complete' without asking a man to become your other half.

Now, no one's suggesting that you approach every relationship with the flexibility and lenience of a 1920s school ma'am. Starting a new relationship and learning about another person also means learning about yourself. Yes, stick to who you are, but accept that a few of your beliefs and preconceptions may be challenged, and be ready for it. After all, the rules that really matter to you will still be there, despite a little challenging.

The real key to new relationships is to go boldly into them. Be strong and be willing to take a little risk now and then, whether that means making the first move or just facing up to your first big night out with all his friends. Try to keep your focus on the situation in hand, and avoid worries about what will happen to the two of you ten years down the line. Focus on the moment, and worry about everything else later.

So now we get to the nitty-gritty. Here come the dating dilemmas. Does he like me? Is he going to make a move? Should I dump him? Etc, etc. This is where you'll find not only a natty explanation of exactly what's going on, but a lot of advice on exactly what you can do about it. After all, there's no point having a long-winded exploration of the deeper psychological basis to his apparent reluctance to let you stay the night, if you're still getting the door slammed in your face every night. Equally, you'll find it far easier to deal with his insane jealousy if you understand where it comes from and why it is happening. So this is the bit where you get to deal with the problem *and* the solution.

Now, of course, *The Man Manual* couldn't possibly deal with *every* single dating problem *every* single woman in the whole world has *ever* experienced. (For fear of resembling the full *Encyclopaedia Britannica* reference library, as opposed to a quick guide). But what it does accomplish is a treatment of some of the man dilemmas most of us have experienced at some point. Who hasn't liked somebody, only to wonder if he feels the same way? Who hasn't felt the dreadful realisation that one half of your amazing new relationship isn't quite as keen as you thought (whether that's your half or his half)? And even if your exact problem isn't outlined here, there's probably something similar that will require the same treatment. So, for example, if your boyfriend is refusing to even contemplate the idea of your first holiday together, despite your ridiculous 'hinting', then he may be displaying the same symptoms as the boyfriend who refuses to introduce you to Mummy and Daddy. So the solutions you find for that problem can often be extremely helpful in dealing with yours. And if you want to cheat (even more), dive straight to the Quick Tips and just pick up the main points. If only everything in life was so straightforward . . .

Q. I like somebody, why isn't he making a move?

Here's what's happening and why

So here's the dilemma. That lunch-break flirting has escalated to a new level, in fact you're pretty sure you can hear collective cringing from just about everybody who is unfortunate enough to witness your smug, cosy, little love bubble. You've made just the right level of physical contact – you've been brushing imaginary hairs off his jacket and touching his arm lightly with each hysterical joke he cracks. And all the signs are there. He always appears as if by magic when he sees you talking to other men. He regularly pops by your desk to see if you want anything from the newsagent's next door. And under extreme duress, largely taking the form of leg-hair pulling, his best friend Steve has admitted that the man in question does indeed have a little 'thing' for you. So why on earth hasn't he asked you on a date? You know you like him and you're pretty sure that he likes you, so what's the problem?

Well, the first issue here is the assumption that it's his problem in the first place. Women often make the mistake of automatically assuming that the first move is strictly male territory. We want equality in politics, business and the bedroom, but in dating? No, thank you. Many of us are more than happy to leave the initiative here firmly in the hands of the boys. It's almost as if we assume that maternity wards across the country welcome the arrival of a little blue bundle with a secret package that includes tools, football statistics and The Comprehensive Guide to How to Woo a Woman! We expect the man to do all the running because, well, he's a man. What we don't account for is the reality that he has exactly the same insecurities as you. Why haven't you taken the plunge and asked him yet? Because you're scared he'll say *no*. And that's fine, but acknowledge that perhaps this forms a big part of his reason for not making that crucial move yet. Just because he's a man doesn't mean he's immune to embarrassment or rejection, or the fear of either two.

Another freebie that unfortunately is not handed out to baby boys, along with the aforementioned paraphernalia, is telepathy. It's all very well admitting to your friends that you spend six hours a day gazing at his personal website, or that his name is now your email password, but it doesn't help him get any closer to the fact that you like him. Because he doesn't know. We spend half our lives complaining that men don't understand the things we do tell them, so how the hell are they supposed to fathom the things we don't? You need to acknowledge that just because you've decided that you'd really like to spend more time with him, it doesn't mean that he knows that.

Here's what to do about it

Now, this doesn't mean that your next step is hiring a sky-writer to declare your feelings, or taking out a thirty-second advertising slot on ITV to tell him and the world just how beautiful your children would be. It just means that you can give a him a little green light. Try and let him know that if he does make a move he won't be knocked back, and then you can share the responsibility a little, rather than expecting him to do all the running. So how do you give this green light? It doesn't necessarily mean throwing yourself across his desk or wearing shorter skirts and brighter, lower necklines. It might just mean paying him a little extra attention, laughing at his jokes a little more confidently. It might mean that once everybody else leaves the room and it's just you and him, you stick around and ask him about what he's up to at the moment, rather than scuttling away. Use the time alone to get to know him better, rather than feeling awkward because it's just the two of you. And flirting is important, in whatever form feels most comfortable to you. Everybody flirts differently. We all have a friend who is blatant, cheeky and often outrageous when flirting. Likewise, everyone knows that girl who is coy, cute and girlie. Flirting doesn't come with a rulebook, so find your own way of letting him know that you're interested. Perhaps try a relaxed smile next time he walks past, rather than your well-practised stare at the floor manoeuvre, which says 'cool and aloof' to you, but 'obsession with the carpet' to him. Be approachable, be friendly and be open to any advances on his part.

Sadly, if we find that he still isn't making that move then we begin to find a million and one different explanations. So, if he hasn't asked you for dinner yet, we tell our friends 'Well, he's clearly married,' or 'He must think I'm married.' Or, even worse, we begin to blame ourselves: 'He hasn't approached me because of my big nose'. Or 'He thinks I'm fat so he's be ashamed to be seen with me.' So, our confidence can take a big knock as we begin to internalise the situation more and more. Of course, he doesn't think your nose is big, and he doesn't think you're fat. These assumptions say far more about us than they do about him. So try not to build up a million explanations for his backwardness in coming forward. Because you'll probably be wrong. And all that will mean is a blow to your confidence that will only hinder your plans to snare the man of your dreams.

If all else fails, and the signs all say that he likes you but he still isn't making the move, then unfortunately, for peace of mind and a little closure on the situation, there is just one solution remaining. OK, take a deep breath. Sit down. And try not to faint with the shock and utter horror of this suggestion. But you could ask him out. Now, providing you're still holding this book and you haven't dropped it in terror of the very suggestion, let's continue. Think about it, we expect men to make these kind of gestures all the time, and very rarely do we credit them with much intelligence, so if he can do it then so can you!

And if he doesn't take you up on your offer? Well, at least you know that you left the door open for him and didn't leave it all up to chance. You gave him the opportunity to make the move, and if he didn't then it's not necessarily a reflection on you. It's far more likely to be a reflection of his current situation or his own insecurities. Or perhaps you simply misread the signs and he just isn't interested. It's not the end of the world. And it just means that you're free to test your new-found flirting tactics and supreme approach strategies on the rest of the men on the planet. Those lucky, lucky men . . .

Sometimes it really is best to just grab that bull (or man, whatever your taste . . .) by the horns and be honest. But with anything in life there is a wrong way and a right way. So how do you step the fine line between envy of the office and prize fool? Well, conveniently, and at the risk of sounding slightly smug, *The Man Manual* can help you out with this one too . . .

QUICK TIPS

1. Imagine yourself as a Bardot-esque sexpot who is, of course, the object of desire for every man in the office, nay, the whole world. But avoid a fake French accent.
2. Wait until you see him begin to pack up for the day. Look distracted and busy, until . . .
3. At the key moment, as he strolls past for his daily goodbye, go for it – ask him if he fancies a quick drink.

Q. How do I tell him I like him?

Here's what's happening and why

Sometimes you just need to get it off your chest. Whether he feels the same or not, you just know you'll feel better once you've told him you like him. In fact, you're actually looking forward to it – even if it means a little rejection – because anything is preferable to sleepless nights, obsessive love-song singing and boring your friends to a point where they want to disown you. And, of course, the best-case scenario is that he might just feel the same way. So you've decided that you just have to tell him. And the decision is the easy part, because now you have to decide exactly how to tell him. And despite banging on about how different men and women are, there are a couple of things where the two sexes definitely agree.

For example, take chat-up lines. When a guy sidles up to you in a nightclub and says, 'Have you got a mirror in your knickers, love, 'cos I can see myself in them!' what's your reaction? Warm graciousness? Charmed laughter? Or repulsed cringing? It's probably the third one, and if it's not then you've definitely been hanging around that night-club far too long . . . When some creep demands you 'Get your coat, you've pulled', your first reaction is probably to get your coat . . . so you can suffocate him with it. So you know that these lines don't work on you, why on earth would they charm him into a lifetime of great sex and loved-up happiness? The crux of the matter is that chat-up lines do not work. They will never be the best way of trying to approach somebody you fancy. This is largely because they are so false. No ordinary person speaks in cheesy riddles and overdone puns. And no matter how original you think your chat-up line is, somebody has always used it before. So, to use an old adage, honesty really is the best policy. But that's far easier said than done. So if you're ready to make the first move, how on earth do you do it?

Here's what to do about it

Just be honest. Be yourself. And be direct. You don't have to march up to him and demand he join you for dinner at 19:00 hours in the nearest pizza restaurant, or else. But don't ask him for a drink and then spend the next five minutes trying to convince him that you're just thirsty, and you have absolutely no romantic intentions concerning him whatsoever, unless of course he feels the same way, which you're sure he doesn't, but you don't mind because you don't even really like him, well of course you like him but just as a friend, and you only asked him for a drink because friends spend time together, and there's nothing wrong with that, so would he like to join you? See, it's confusing.

Be casual and relaxed. Ask if he wants to go for a coffee. See if he has any plans for the weekend. Remember the composed, confident, charming woman you are with friends, around family and when trying to get refunds in expensive shops, and try to be her. Your suggestion should be enough to give him a little clue that you might just like him, without constituting a grand declaration of love. And it really isn't as scary as it sounds. Making the first move doesn't have to be a big speech about what he means to you, how long you've liked him and exactly what you'd like to do to him. Make the approach light, relaxed and welcoming, and (a) he's far more likely to accept, and (b) you're far less likely to come off as nervous wreck.

Bear in mind how often you see this man because that will have an influence on the best way to ask him out. If you only ever see him when you're out with a particular group of friends every few months, then why not go for it and ask if he wants to meet for lunch sometime? What have you got to lose? However, if you see him everyday at work then perhaps a more subtle approach would be best. Whilst courage and risk-taking are certainly qualities to be admired, nobody wants to be 'that girl from the office who asked Mark on a ten-day holiday to the Caribbean'. Stick with a gentle invite to grab a mid-morning coffee. Also, if he does turn down the offer, you'll feel far less embarrassed if it was a casual, breezy suggestion, rather than a full-blown marriage proposal.

And if he says, 'No, thanks.' Fine. If your offer has been suitably relaxed, the refusal won't feel like too much of a rejection. Retain the composed, charming etc., etc. front, and say, 'Well, maybe another time,' and stroll off. Don't have a tantrum, at least not in front of him (tantrums in the toilet with the girls afterwards are always acceptable).

QUICK TIPS

1. Be cool, calm, collected and any other words beginning with 'c' that convey the impression of confidence. (See, there's another one.)
2. If necessary, accept rejection graciously.
3. Remember to check your teeth for remnants of lunch before you begin, it's really never the best turn on . . .

Q. Why doesn't he call when he says he's going to?

Here's what's happening and why

When we say, 'Thank you for a lovely evening,' normally we mean it. When we say, 'I'd love to see you again,' we nearly always mean it. OK, when we say, 'I'm so sorry, I'm about to move to Uzbekistan,' or 'Your career in post-it note packing is so fascinating!' we might be stretching the truth a little, but on the whole we won't go to the effort of sounding more interested in a guy than we are. We know the accepted signals and what they stand for. If he asks to see you tomorrow night, that's a good sign. If he wants to introduce you to his family – good sign. If he drops you at the end of your road and makes you walk the rest – bad sign. If he excuses himself to use the gents and doesn't return – very bad sign. Upon going your own separate ways after a great date, if he says, 'I'll call you' – good sign, right? Well, you would think so. But here we come across one of the dating world's most confusing conundrums. He's capable of reducing the most 'together' women to screaming, hair-pulling levels of frustration. Ladies, this is the guy who says he will call and never ever does. No amount of staring at the phone will help. No amount of voodoo chanting or willing him to make that call will make the slightest bit of difference. And so you make up excuses. Maybe, just after you said goodbye, a flock of killer pigeons flew by and snatched your number from his pocket. Or maybe he was the victim of an obscure burglary and his home phone was taken. Maybe there is an oddity with BT's lines that means that his number can never connect to yours. Maybe he's had a nasty accident and he's in hospital. Maybe it was the killer pigeons. After exhausting every possibility and finally admitting to yourself, your prematurely excited mother and your girls that actually he just isn't going to call ever, you find yourself, like a million women before you, asking, 'Why did he say he was going to call, if he never intended to?'

'I'll call you' has become a massive dating cliché. In the Dating Cliché Hall of Fame (really, it exists), it's up there with 'It's not you, it's me' (which can be roughly translated as 'It's not me, it's you') and 'I just need some space' (which can usually be translated as 'Get the hell out of my life, I'm sick of you'). In fact, the presence of an 'I'll call you', far from spreading optimism in a new relationship, can be a verbal kiss of death. Most of us would rather a polite goodnight and goodbye, with no empty promises and no 'I'll call you's.' At least you're not phone-hanging for the next three weeks.

And the trouble is that an 'I'll call you' gives the person uttering it a lot of power. Because, of course, once he's said it you can't possibly call him because that would be too keen, so you have no choice but to wait. And wait. And wait. And throw a few things around in a rage. And wait. And wait. Meanwhile the non-caller has forgotten all about his idle promise and has probably moved on to a new plethora of ladies that he can wine, dine and leave confused. So why on earth do men do it? Its simple, we just want them to say they'll call, and call, or not bother with any of it. Why are men so fond of the 'I'll call you' when most of the time they don't even mean it?

Well, as we said before, men are often expected to do all the running when it comes to initiating a new relationship. They're the ones who are expected to make all the moves. Generally, they take more chances than women do, so this means that, due to the facts of probability, they usually experience rejection more than woman. In fact, you could say that, compared to women, men are experts at rejection. And this means that they try to be a little more sympathetic when it's their turn to do the rejecting. So, for a man, 'I'll call you' is often seen as a get-out clause, and as far as he's considered it's a damn sight kinder than sitting you down and explaining in a painfully-long monologue the exact reasons why you're just not 'the one'. Also, as mentioned before, men are less comfortable than women with discussing their feelings and emotions. So, really, saying, 'I'll call you' is far easier than saying, 'Actually, I won't call you' even though, more often than not, that is what he means. It allows him to escape unscathed from the situation and move on to the next. No confrontation, no discussion and minimal effort. And just as problems in relationships often occur because we expect him to behave like us, the problem here is that he is seeing the situation through a man's eyes and expecting you to see it the same way. He would far rather be rejected in this casual, non-confrontational manner, so he assumes that you will see things this way too. Of course, he underestimates the female need for answers and reasoning, so this paves the way for a lot of confusion. In short, it helps to learn that 'I'll call you', in most cases, means 'I will never call you because I'm not interested, but it's far easier to say I'll call than explain all this to you.' So pop that one in your male-female translation handbook.

Here's what to do about it

So how do you deal with this then? How do you avoid falling into the 'I'll call you' trap? There are two things you can do really. Firstly, make it clear that you really aren't interested in him saying he'll call if he has no intention of doing just that. You don't have to say this in as many words, but you can convey the impression of somebody who is approaching the relationship in a casual, relaxed manner. What's more, you could actually approach the relationship in this way. If you're on a good date then don't become preoccupied with whether or not he's likely to call tomorrow, enjoy the moment and the chances are that he probably will call. Let him know that you don't need him to make you promises like 'I'll call you' to keep you happy, you're fine without them. If he calls, then great – if he doesn't, then that's fine too.

Secondly, and probably most effectively, take control of the situation. At the end of the evening, simply say, 'Thank you, I've had a lovely time. I'll call you sometime in the week.' And, instantly, the ball is in your court, and you can decide whether you want to volley it back or let it bounce out of play. Equally, you won't spend the next three days screaming, 'He hasn't called! He hasn't called! He hasn't called!' because *he's* waiting for *you* to call. It means that you can pick a moment when you are feeling suitably chatty, flirty and confident, rather than him catching you when you're trying to brush your teeth, pull your tights on and straighten your hair simultaneously. You'll feel far more relaxed and if you still get the impression, after speaking to him, that he really isn't interested, then so be it. What have you lost? At least you had the chance to play things out in your own time, rather than waiting by a phone that just won't ring.

QUICK TIPS

1. Don't reply to 'I'll call you' with 'Don't lie to me, you feeble, pathetic loser.'
2. Don't hover at the front door until he says 'I'll call you.' Leave it in the hands of fate.
3. Take his number; tell him *you'll* call *him*. Take control and save on the stress.

Q. Why does he want to rush into sex so quickly?

Here's what's happening and why

Of course, in the movies, everybody wants sex at the same time. All it takes is a glance between Brad Pitt and a lucky leading lady, after a particularly exhausting, yet adrenalin-pumping car chase, and there are bras a-flying, muscles a-rippling and legs akimbo. And, of course, it's absolutely mind-blowing. For both of them. And the postcoital action doesn't consist of a deep chat about where the relationship's going. And he doesn't think she's a moaning old prude, and she doesn't think he's got a one-track mind. But we all know that life just ain't like the movies. And, in reality, the chances that you and him will both feel ready for sex at the same stage are fairly slim. While you want to chat about what film to see at the weekend, he'll be trying to discreetly knock your bra strap off your shoulder. While you're enjoying a cosy, warm kiss and cuddle, he'll be silently hoping that it might just lead to something more. The fact is that different people feel comfortable with varying levels of intimacy at different stages. And also we are conditioned to think that sex is only acceptable at a certain stage of the relationship. So there are all sorts of pressures on us to pick the perfect moment to go that step further.

Whatever other uncertainties you come across in your attempts to negotiate the big sex question, you can be sure of one thing: he will see it entirely differently to you. Sex is one of the most basic functions the human body performs, so why is it so complicated? Well, this is mainly because men and women see sex so differently. You know how you really feel like you're going somewhere when he first calls you his girlfriend or holds your hand? Perhaps the first time he cooks for you is a big step? You feel like you've achieved something. And this can be the way he feels about sex. The first time he manages to get you into bed can be a big deal to him because he has almost won the competition he has set up in his head. It sounds like the dreaded notches-on-the-bedpost scenario, and that's probably because it is, in essence. To him, sex might be like a goal, an accomplishment, and everytime you knock him back it just makes him want it more. Also, a lot of men show emotion through sex. They are far more physical than women, and while we often assume that men do not attach any emotion to sex, in fact it can be closely linked with their self-esteem, manly prowess and pride. So sex isn't just about proving something to you, it's about proving something to himself.

Also, the circumstances of your relationship might influence when you feel ready for sex. Where did you meet? If it was ten years ago at school and your relationship has gradually developed from a genuine friendship into a tentative romance, then your relationship is likely to hinge on a number of things, not just your sex life. However, if your first words to each other consisted of sexy flirting while you grinded each other to an R. Kelly song in a sweaty nightclub, then sex and the sexual attraction between you might form a bigger part of your bond. Research has found that men view women they meet in bars and clubs as casual sex partners rather than marriage material. If you marketed yourself as a saucy sex kitten to catch his attention, you can empathise with his misunderstanding that sex is your main priority. While this doesn't give him a licence to demand sex, it can explain his attitude to when you should be getting it on.

Here's what to do about it

Look at the two separate agendas going on here. Why is there such a big difference in terms of when you feel ready for sex? If he's ready, why aren't you? Look at your reasons. If waiting a while longer is just one of your boundaries then make that point. Loud and clear. Make sure there are no misunderstandings and inform him that there will be absolutely no sex until you feel you know him a bit better. If he's worth sticking with he'll understand. If you don't feel ready then tell him that, and explain that it's just not something you feel comfortable with.

Dating dilemmas can often be dealt with by making subtle gestures and gentle hints. Not this one. Get straight to the point. After all, you are talking about the most basic biological function there is, you are referring to the possibility or the non-possibility of the two of you rolling around naked together. So subtlety doesn't really come into it. Just say, 'I really like you, but I don't feel ready for that yet. I hope you understand.' Simple as that. It saves on a lot of awkward moments with him thinking 'Is she ready yet?' and you thinking 'Get off!' Don't make him feel like a serial sex pest for trying. Perhaps he just thought you wanted him to take the initiative – lots of women do. Once you've cleared up the situation with him he'll probably be grateful, at least he knows you that your reticence isn't because his breath smells, or something similar.

But just as we can feel pressured into having sex, we can also feel pressured to not have sex. Whilst you're doing your sex-related soul searching, you might discover that actually you do trust him and you do want to have sex with him. So what's stopping you? Well, you've always been told that it'll never go anywhere if you let him have it too soon. Your mum's telling you to wait. Your friends are telling you to wait. But you don't feel that you want to. Going with what you feel is right doesn't make you easy, so if everything is telling you that this is the right thing to do, but you're concerned about what everyone else will think, then you need to learn to challenge that.

It's your relationship and as much as your mother and your friends and the magazines you read mean well, they can't read the situation as well as you can, so don't be led or feel guilty.

Whatever decision you and him make about sex, just make sure that you both make the decision on your own terms and that there is no pressure involved. Don't sacrifice your boundaries for him. Equally, he shouldn't feel that he is doing anything he doesn't want to do. Make sure you are informed, sure and honest, and you will both feel like you're playing an equal part in the progression.

QUICK TIPS

1. The decision is yours, either way.
2. Be frank, if you're going to get naked with this person you need to be able to look them in the eye and tell them straight too.
3. If he doesn't understand your decision, he's about as much good to you as that crotchless thong he bought you. Say goodbye.

Q. Why does he get so touchy about me sleeping over?

Here's what's happening and why

So you think things are going swimmingly, you're having a fantastic time. He loves your friends, they love him. He dresses well, dances well and kisses like an expert. He laughs at your jokes and thinks your weird little habits are 'cute'. He treats you with respect, affection and kindness.

He's an open book who wears his heart on his sleeve, so you feel you can talk to him about anything. Until you turn up at his door with a toothbrush. And you simply can't fathom out why a five-inch hygiene tool with bristles could strike such strength of feeling in your usually brave, composed new boyfriend. 'What's that?' he stutters. 'Well,' you begin, 'it's a toothbrush.' A pause. Terrified confusion still apparent. 'I, erm . . . use it to brush my teeth. I just hate that scummy teeth feeling in the morning!' You smile, he doesn't. Instead his next contribution is 'The morning?' 'Yes,' you volunteer as you find yourself on the verge of answering another ridiculously unnecessary question. 'It's that time between night-time and lunchtime . . . I thought I could stay.'

To you, this makes sense. After all, you've been having cosy nights in until four in the morning, and it's such an effort to drag yourself home then, so surely it's easier all round if you just stay? Apparently not. 'Erm, actually I've got work early tomorrow, why don't we just go out for something to eat, and then I'll drop you home . . . take your toothbrush with you, no, don't leave it here . . . there's no, erm, room for it.' So, of course, the rest of the night is spent in a strange limbo as you try to work out what the hell's got into him, and he tries to work out why his girlfriend has suddenly turned up the pressure on the relationship.

This comes back to the fact that women and men are conditioned to view relationships differently. Years ago, and we're not talking about the seventies here, men were supposed to be sowing seeds all over the place and racking up notches on the bedpost in order to ensure the survival of the species. To an extent, many men still feel that being tied to one woman is binding and restricting, and many women feel that they should be striving for a relationship. And these two agendas often contradict one another.

Here's what to do about it

In this situation, look at the evidence. This is his home, his pad, his space. And while he may be more than happy to spend hours with you, when you turn up with a toothbrush he's likely to feel that his solitary environment could be threatened. To you, perhaps, it's just a toothbrush. But to him, that tiny little instrument can be as symbolic as a wedding ring. You might as well have turned up and chained yourself to his ankle. And while women are often accused of blowing things out of proportion, men can be guilty too. Perhaps you're not trying to weasel your way further into his life, but you really just do hate that furry-teeth sensation. Perhaps his place is closer to where you work. Perhaps your flatmate is having a huge party tonight and you want to stay away. Before you begin explaining all of this to him, you need to try and suss out exactly why he is so touchy about sleepovers.

It could be that he just isn't ready for that step and it freaks him out a little bit. Now, this is all very well if you feel that you're not quite at the matching bathrobes stage either. But if you are, and you can't quite understand his reservations, then this is something you need to talk about it. If you really get the impression that he feels a little scared about you marching round, pyjamas in a rucksack, then perhaps you do need to place your reasons in a practical context. If he's feeling that you want too much, too soon, then bleating, 'But I really want to be able to smell your skin and caress your earlobes all night! I need to be close to you!' isn't really going to help. Explain that it's easier to get to work, or about your housemate's party, and it will help him to realise that you're not launching a single-handed invasion of his bachelor pad.

And you never know, perhaps it's not the sleepovers that he has an issue with. Perhaps it's the fact that he hasn't been asked or consulted that makes him feel a little uneasy. He might just feel that important relationship decisions are being made without him, when in actual fact you really haven't put that much thought into it. Little misunderstandings like this can seem monumental until you talk about them, so it really is best to get them out in the open. Basically, you both need to be clear about exactly what spending the night together means to both of you. If there are differences in what you want in this department, then communication is vital to establish how important these differences are and whether you feel comfortable compromising them.

QUICK TIPS

1. Don't turn up with a 160kg suitcase and an Ikea catalogue. If he's anxious about you weasling your way into his life, at least make sure you do it subtly.
2. Sometimes, tell him that he can't stay at yours because you're busy or you need your space. Remind him you're just as keen to hold on to your life as he is.
3. Don't attempt any painting, decorating or impulsive DIY while he's at work. Trust me, it won't be a 'nice surprise'.

Q. Why is he so jealous of my male friends?

Here's what's happening and why

When you begin a new relationship, there are a number of 'firsts' you have to encounter. For example, the first time he stays at yours, the first time you hold hands in public, the first time he calls you his girlfriend and the first time you send a joint card. There are set rites of passage that every fledgling couple goes through on the journey to full-on togetherness. And there's a sense of relief and comfort once you've negotiated your way through each of these little challenges. One of the more nerve-racking of these firsts is meeting each other's friends. It's always a little scary meeting his crowd. How do you know that his girls aren't super-bitches from hell? How do you know that his mates aren't a bunch of boring old men who'll talk business all day, leaving you out in the cold? Or worse, they could be a bunch of louts who'll try to force-feed you lager and pinch your bum. Yes, meeting his friends is always an experience greeted with a little trepidation, no matter how wonderful they turn out to be. But your friends? Well, of course, he will love, love, love your crowd. How could he not? You smile fondly at the little bunch you have acquired through a lifetime of charmed memories, with firm confidence that the new man will love them as much as you do.

Except, you get home and he keeps making snidey comments about Steve's muscles and Tom's flashy car. Karen's 'a bit loud' and Sara's 'a bit smutty'. In fact, he has something negative to say about all of your friends. He accuses a couple of 'blatantly fancying you'. And suddenly the wonderful scenarios you had built up in your head of long lazy days spent with your boyfriend and your mates look a little blurry. Then, everytime you mention that you're heading out for a drink with the crowd you sense the tension. 'Oh, really?' he says. If he were a cat he'd be arching his back and spitting. If he were a dog, he'd probably be urinating all over you, just in case the boys get any funny ideas about exactly whose territory you are. Why do men get so jealous of your friends when they are just that?

Well, meeting a partner's friends can be a confusing task. Because while asking polite questions about jobs, homes and cars, there is a whole new level of investigation operating at the same time. So as you hear your beloved asking your mate if he watched the rugby last night, inside his head he may well be asking, 'Has he ever slept with my girlfriend?' He's trying to work out exactly what these people mean to you. To an extent it is a competition, because he wants to know: do these guys mean more to her than me? Do they know her better than me? Have they ever seen her naked? It's easy when you meet family, you know exactly who everyone is and what their relation to you is. And if you really can't work it out, they've all got labels – brother, uncle, father. Friendship groups can be much harder to fathom.

Also, there are still a lot of men (and women) who believe that it is impossible for men and women to be just friends. If he's one of them, then when you see a healthy, platonic friendship, he'll see a man desperately trying to get into his girlfriend's knickers. This could be a reflection of his own relationships with women. If he has a strong group of female friends, then he's likely to understand your friendships with the boys. If, however, he's only ever bothered getting to know girls that he wants to sleep with, then you can see why he might be suspicious of your friendships. So what does this mean then? Are you destined to lead a double life, in two separate dimensions, where your friends and your boyfriend must never, ever meet? Well, not necessarily. There are some ways for you to address the problem.

Here's what to do about it

Firstly, you can help by clearing up some of the confusion. If you sense that he's concerned about exactly how close you and one of your male friends are, then make it plainly obvious that you are just friends. To you, it may be obvious, but if it isn't to him then it might help him feel at ease if you re-assert the status of the friendship. That doesn't mean that you have to play down the friendship, if your friends are critically important to you then that's fine, tell him that, but try and make it clear how he fits into that too. Understand that in his mind he's probably invented false fantasies of you and John, or you and Steve rolling around together in fits of passion (regardless of how unattractive the idea is to you!) You can take away these fantasies by talking about what great friends these boys are, and how you see them more like brothers, for example.

Also, you can make sure that he doesn't feel left out of your friendship circle. If your relationships with male friends are causing problems, then try to make sure you don't combat this by just ensuring that the two parties never meet. It may well be easier to meet with your mates on your own because when he's there you know he feels uncomfortable, but restricting yourself to 'boyfriend time' and 'friend time' will only make him feel more left out. Also, if he's not there, those fantasies about exactly what you're getting up to will only thrive. And, it will be a bigger issue when you say, 'I'm going to the pub with the guys,' if he knows those plans don't include him. So, although it may be awkward at first, try and integrate spending time with your male friends and spending time with your boyfriend.

Women are often seen as the more sociable sex, but it's amazing what can happen when you leave a group of guys, who don't know each other, alone. When socialising with your male friends and your boyfriend, don't feel like you have to hold his hand the whole way through. If anything, he'll bond far better with the boys when you're not there, if not for any other reason – just out of necessity. When you're around he'll probably let you do the bulk of the chatting – particularly if he feels uncomfortable, after all they're your friends. So when you pop to the ladies, take a little longer, leave him on his own for a bit. It'll give him a chance to get to know your friends for himself without a running commentary from you. OK, so six-hour toilet trips may raise a little concern, and downright suspicion, but use any time you can excuse yourself to give him a chance to find out exactly why your friends are so important to you.

QUICK TIPS

1. Don't ever compare your male friends to your boyfriend, in terms of job prospects, the car they drive or anything else.

2. Try not to break arrangements with your man to meet your friends, if it can be avoided. He'll feel like he's coming second-best.

3. Find an interest that your boyfriend and your friends have in common, and capitalise. Even if it means attending three live tiddlywinks championships within the space of a month. Anything to bring them closer . . .

Q. Why is he so competitive?

Here's what's happening and why

When something really great happens in your life, you want everybody to know. You want to shout it from the rooftops, whether it be passing your degree with flying colours, securing your dream job or even just squeezing into that size ten dress you've lusted after for months. You ring your mum, your friends and fight the temptation to take out a full-page ad in a local, no – a national newspaper. So why do you feel like you can't enjoy your success with quite the same relish when you are with your boyfriend? Perhaps he's having a tough time at work and doesn't want to hear about your fabulous promotion. Maybe he's a little hard up for cash at the moment and celebrating with an all-expenses-paid (by you) meal is his worst nightmare. It can be easy to dismiss his reticence as plain jealousy. But, it can also be really disheartening when you feel that you can't celebrate your success with the one person who means the most to you. So why is he so competitive? And how can you deal with this and move on?

Well, by nature we are all slightly competitive. We all want to strive to reach our ideals. And let's face it, it was probably your competitive streak that got you that great promotion in the first place. To an extent, competition can be healthy, but in a relationship it can be disastrous because it pits you against each other when really you should be striving together. One of the joys of being in a relationship is the ability to share the highs and lows with each other. When he's doing really well, you want to feel proud and you want to enjoy his success. And when you're doing well, you want him to feel the same way. You don't want to go out for a celebratory meal and spend the whole night trying to ignore his sulky, wincing face. You want to know why he can't accept your success.

For a start, men have become increasingly confused in recent years over exactly what and who we want them to be. Do we want them to swashbuckle into our lives and assume the role of provider, protector and general door-opener? (And risk getting slapped or lectured on equal rights.) Or do we want him to don a sarong, grow his hair and become a caring, sharing lover, friend and companion? (And risk getting, at best, called a wimp and at worst getting completely ridiculed) 'New man', 'new lad' and the 'ladette' have all contributed to a general confusion over whether he should drink more than you, earn more than you or wear more make-up than you. A recent poll found that most men (and women) still think that women are more attracted to men with more money. The poll also revealed that more than half of men feel that they should be the main breadwinner within a relationship. So traditionally-assigned gender stereotypes are still present in our society. And this could have implications for your relationship.

Here's what to do about it

Well, to start with, bear these stereotypes in mind. Consider how this makes him feel when he has to ask to borrow a tenner to fill up his car, or you are paying for dinner again. Like many issues within relationships, the ideas we have been socialised into believing can become big problems because they are so hard to shift. If he thinks you and society want him to be a provider, he might find it hard to celebrate the pay rise that takes you sailing ahead of him in terms of your pay cheques.

But you won't apologise for your success, and you shouldn't, so you need to find a way to make him see your relationship less like a competition and more like a partnership. Take it into your own hands to establish the boundaries of your relationship. Explain that your success is not something that you want compared to his. It is something that you want to celebrate with him, just like you expect to be able to share in all his success because you are proud of him. Explain that you are concerned that you won't be able to support one another if there is an underlying sense of competition. Tell him that you want to play on the same team as him, and not against him.

And try to make him a part of your success. Remember all those times he proof-read your reports in the dead of the night and corrected millions of errors, and make sure he knows that you couldn't have achieved it without him. Tell him about how you would never have completed that mini-marathon if he hadn't come training with you everyday for six months, come rain or shine. And remind him that you earning more than him only means that you can achieve joint goals such as that new house or a dog a little quicker. Let him know that you truly, genuinely believe that he will achieve all of the goals he has set himself.

And concentrate on projects that really are shared efforts, whether that's painting the shed, renovating his old car or house-training your new puppy. Focusing on things that you can achieve with each other will take the heat off your individual achievements and set up a co-operative sense in your relationship. Let him know you need to work with him and not against him.

QUICK TIPS

1. Do not tell him that he can't choose where you eat, what you eat and where you go 'because you don't pay for it'.
2. If you must buy him things, then buy him treats not necessities. If you buy him a nice new shirt or a new computer game, you'll feel like a generous girlfriend. If you buy him pants and socks, you'll feel like his mother.
3. When you do well, thank him for his contributions. Look at it as a joint success, not 'your success'.

Q. Why does he want to sleep with me, but not date me?

Here's what's happening and why

So, the sex is great. Physically, you're content. He's great looking, he's fun to be with and he's an expert in bed. And he seems to be pretty in to you too. After all, he's always telling you how sexy you are, he always wants you to come over and he even bought you some gorgeous lingerie the other day. Brilliant. Apart from there are a few little niggling things that you just can't seem to get your head round. Like the way you only ever spend time at his flat or yours in bed. Like the way you've never met any of his friends or family. The way you never go on dates. The way you really don't appear to be moving any closer to being a real couple. It can hit pretty hard when you realise that he sees your relationship completely differently to you. So what do you do when you want the closeness you share in the bedroom to move outside the bedroom? You like him, he's perfect boyfriend material, so how do you secure him as your boyfriend?

Well, the truth of it is that you might not be able to. And it's not really his fault. As harsh as it sounds, for a man who isn't ready to commit, sex without strings is not a prelude to a relationship – it's just having his cake and eating it. Every time he's drunk, bored or just up for it. If he isn't willing to welcome you into any other part of his life than his bedroom, and you keep sleeping with him minus any other sign of commitment, then you only really have yourself to blame. As much as screaming, 'He used me, the #*@!*ing *#*!#*@!' might make you feel better, the reality is that he only used you because you let him. Think about it, if somebody said you could have an un-limited supply of Judith Leiber handbags, or Manolo Blahnik shoes, or Tiffany diamonds for an unspecified period, with no price to pay and no commitment to the deal, you'd make the most of it while you could. You'd be working those accessories, dripping in diamonds. And if you're sleeping with somebody who hasn't made any commitment to you, then this is the kind of deal you're effectively making.

Here's what to do about it

Now, of course, you might be fine with this. You might not be looking for a solution. If you see him as someone who stimulates you physically, but who really doesn't fit your life partner criteria, then that's fine. Go for it. Perhaps you just enjoy the companionship and the sex, perhaps you're really not looking for a relationship so the deal works out just fine for you. Equally, there's no need to feel guilty about this. For years, men have been getting away with treating sex as functional, while women have been desperately trying to attach some emotional importance. So why shouldn't you value sex as just that – sex? There is no shame in wanting just that from him, so don't feel pressured by a society that conditions women into believing that wanting to sleep with a man without wanting to marry him is dirty. Challenge the rules that say 'nice girls just don't'. As long as you feel respected and content, then who cares what your mother's generation thinks?

If, however, you don't feel respected and you don't feel that you are getting what you want from the relationship, then there's only one real way to deal with it. If you've tested the water and you're getting definite 'just sex' vibes, then you need to call it off. If you're unhappy now, hanging around, continuing to sleep with him really won't make you feel any better. It won't convince him to commit. Who knows, once you show him that you're clear about demanding a more serious commitment by leaving, he may well realise that you mean more to him than just sex. And if he doesn't? Well, you've lost nothing. Just sex is fine if that's all you want, but if it's not and it's still all you're getting then you need to make a clean break. By sticking around and letting him bond with you in the bedroom, but not outside it, all you're doing is handing him a licence to disrespect you. And it's your fault as much as it is his. So make a move, and go and find what you really deserve.

QUICK TIPS

1. Trying to talk to him seriously about your 'future' while still wearing your see-through bra, chocolate body paint and handcuffs probably won't work.

2. If it is just sex, then make sure he is still treating you with respect. After all, you have simply made a decision that you feel works best for you.

3. Find out if he has the same arrangement with anyone else, because if he does that's a pretty clear indication that he probably doesn't want to take things any further.

Q. I'm in love with my best friend. How do I tell him?

What's happening and why

He's funny. He's sexy. He's polite. He's kind. In fact, your best friend is perfect. But just not for you. Or so you thought. For years your mum has been begging you to ditch your greasy boyfriends with their slick cars and slick hair, and just go out with your best friend because 'He's such a lovely boy!' People in shops assume you're a couple, even when the reason that you're shopping together is because you want him to help you pick a lovely outfit for your amazing date on Saturday night. Even your friends, those who know you best, have occasionally discussed what a great couple you would make. In fact, the only people who can't see you and him together are you and him. After all, he watches you shave your legs, pluck your eyebrows and study your cellulite. He knows your very worst habits. And you don't care because that's what friends are for. Until it hits you. Like a carefully targeted bolt from the blue, you suddenly realise that perhaps they're all right. After all, he is everything you want in a man. You feel relaxed around him, he makes you laugh, he makes you feel secure and there's no denying that he's gorgeous. So what are you waiting for? What do you do next?

Well, making drastic changes to carefully formed friendships is always dangerous territory. One awkward conversation can ruin years of friendship. So the very first thing you need to establish, before you decide to tell your best friend that you'd like to take things a little further, is why you feel this way in the first place. If you didn't see him as a romantic prospect before, why has he suddenly become one? Be very wary if circumstances have suddenly changed in your life. Perhaps your closest girl friend has just got married? Perhaps you've moved away from home and you feel a little lonely? Or maybe he's just got a new girlfriend and you feel that you don't see each other enough any more.

If you're feeling insecure or lonely then this might be the reason that you're seeing your friend in a new light. And it's understandable. After all, if you're such great friends then there's probably a mutual affection and genuine closeness. Which is great, but these things do not a relationship make. If you initiate a relationship purely on the grounds that he's reliable and supportive, then somewhere along the line you will feel like you're missing out on other things. If it's comfort, constant affection and security you want, then get a dog – don't start proclaiming undying love for your best mate.

Before you begin to pour your heart out, you need to do a little emotional homework. Do your background research. Yes, you feel a certain way, but why? Imagine if your girlfriends were all single. Would you still want to enter into a serious relationship with him? Maybe, despite your protests, you can't quite help but wonder if everyone was right and you would be a perfect couple? Maybe he's moved on and you're panicking a little that the option's been taken away from you by his new blonde buxom girlfriend? So imagine she wasn't around and he was still all yours – would you be interested in anything more? Maybe you've just come out of a passionate, tempestuous relationship and you just want something more stable? Ask yourself if your best friend really possesses the qualities that made you feel so strongly about the last boyfriend. Be honest with yourself, because if you get this wrong and misinterpret your feelings, you could end up hurting both parties involved. It's not so much soul searching that you need to do, but soul investigating, grilling and probing. Make sure you're sure before you make the leap, and then, whatever the outcome, at least you know that you've been true to yourself.

Here's what to do about it

And if, after all of that soul searching, you really, genuinely feel that he could just be the one for you, then finding the way to tell him this could be a whole new chapter.

Because it's not the same as approaching a stranger and handing him your telephone number. It's not even the same as asking that hot guy at work to join you for coffee. Because not only do you have to consider your past, you also have to consider your future. You have to be wary, too, of the possibility that these new feelings may just be one-sided. He might see your friendship in exactly the same way as he always has, and your newest confession might come as a bit of a shock. The bonus of having him as a best friend is that you'll probably feel more comfortable being entirely honest with him than you would with another guy. Use this to your advantage and be straight with him. Tell him what you've been thinking and how you would like things to progress.

And a final note. If he feels the same way and you do decide to give it a go, be realistic and sensible about the outcome. Go into it boldly and genuinely, but be realistic enough to establish what will happen if things go wrong. Where will you go back to? How does the friendship recover? It might sound about as romantic as Catherine Zeta-Jones's prenuptial agreement, but discussing the consequences of a relationship could save on a few problems later.

QUICK TIPS

1. If this situation happens within a tight-knit group of friends, make sure he finds out about your feelings from you, and you alone. Gossip can be a real relationship-killer!
2. Don't be convinced by anyone else that you two should be together. Listen to your own instincts.

3. Be sure, because there's a risk that once you've made the jump, it might be hard to go back to the way things were.

Q. Why is he such a flirt when he says he likes me?

Here's what's happening and why

They say 'Hell hath no fury like a woman scorned.' Well Hell would be pretty pushed to come up with a fury that compares to a woman whose boyfriend is flirting with the barmaid too. Why does he have to call her 'darling' and laugh at her ridiculously flirty jokes? Why can't he see that that bitch at his work obviously wants to mother his children? Why on earth does he insist on saving his best jokes for that woman at the petrol station that you know he fancies (three fill-ups in a week is excessive by anybody's standards)? In fact, why can't he just live in a cage to which the only key is held by you?

OK, maybe you don't really want that. But what you do want is to know why he flirts so much and what it really means. Well, the first clue is your reaction. You might well be seething, complaining to your friends about his inability to relocate his eye contact from breasts to face with other women, and you might give him the cold shoulder when he insists on showing off his new moves to random girls on the dancefloor, but unless you tell him what's really going on, then he hasn't got a hope of getting it right. So the first reason for his flirting might just be that you've never told him not to flirt. So whereas you may have invested in a chastity belt and thrown away your pulling pants, you can't expect him to adapt his behaviour to mirror yours unless you talk to him about exactly what you expect. His flirting is probably harmless. He's being the 'him' that he was when you met him, and you seemed to like that 'him' so he's carrying on. He's being a little flirty and outgoing because that's just the way he's always been.

Don't object to the flirting on principle. Don't say, 'I don't want him dancing with other women because people might think he's not that into me,' if you feel OK with it. It can be very healthy if you both feel free to indulge in some harmless flirting. After all, there's nothing more flattering than seeing a gorgeous girl chatting up your boyfriend when you can see he's saying, 'Thanks, but no thanks. I've got a lovely girlfriend who means the world to me.' Equally, seeing you flirting a little can remind him that you're with him because you want to be, not because there's nobody else interested. It's really healthy if you view fun flirting in this way, but if you feel that it's more serious or it is really making you feel uncomfortable, then you do need to address it.

Here's what to do about it

Telling him that you don't feel right when he is so flirty with other women will probably solve the problem. If he's flirting because you've never told him not to, then a quiet word may well be all it takes to let him know that he needs to adapt his behaviour. Just say, 'I felt a little uncomfortable when you spent so much time talking to that girl who approached you in the pub today.' If you can clarify exactly what you object to and what your ideal is, and you are reasonable, then he should make every effort to meet these expectations.

But what if it continues? Despite your quiet word in his shell-like, he's still swapping smutty exchanges with a girl from work, and sending and receiving text messages that dangerously tightrope-walk the line between friendly and flirty. Then you really need to refer back to your own personal set of boundaries of what you will and will not accept. Explain to him that, to you, flirting is linked to respect, and when he flirts so obviously with other women he is showing you a lack of respect. If you've decided that you simply do not feel comfortable watching him schmooze other ladies, then don't settle for anything less. And let him know that you really can't tolerate it. If he has any consideration for your feelings then the message should be beginning to hit home by now, and you should see a change in his behaviour. Be very wary of issuing bold ultimatums such as 'If I catch you looking down one more cleavage, I'll pack my bags', or 'If you flirt anymore, you're dumped', unless you really do mean them. Ultimatums can serve as very good deterrents if he gets the impression you really will leave unless his behaviour changes. But be honest about your own ability to follow the threat through. If you know that you would never be able to leave him over flirting, then don't say it. If you continue the relationship after an ignored ultimatum, you'll feel far worse about the situation, and even worse, he'll know that your threats are empty so he's far more likely to ignore them in the future.

And once you get to this stage, you need to be honest with yourself about the type of relationship you're in. If you've asked him more than once to curb his cheesy lines and too-cosy cuddling, and he carries on regardless, then perhaps you need to question his commitment to the relationship. If the flirting genuinely bothers you and you've made this clear to him, yet he still continues, then you need to evaluate how highly he prioritises your feelings. If 'harmless' flirting is more important to him than your happiness, then are you sure you're actually with the right man anyway?

QUICK TIPS

1. There's flirting and then there's touching. Make sure he knows the difference.
2. Don't try to deal with your feelings about his flirting by attempting to seduce every man in the bar you're in. Two wrongs don't make a healthy relationship.
3. Keep the ultimatums to a minimum: in the end, they only put you in a weaker position.

Q. Why can't I get him to commit?

Here's what's happening and why

Some men say that 'commitment-phobia' doesn't exist. But then, these are the men who are happily married and who love Sundays at home with the kids. And they've probably forgotten that they were once commitment-phobes themselves. The reality is that many women are battling with men whose only apparent commitment is to being single. The median age of first-time marriage for American men currently stands at 27. That's the oldest in history. So it's not just you and your friends, the facts are speaking for themselves. A recent study concluded that there are ten main reasons why men won't commit. These included the ability to get sex easily without marriage, the financial threat of divorce and the desire to own a house before they get a wife. Brilliant. Oh, and in case he needed any more reasons to stay resolutely single, apparently they fear that marriage will require too many changes and compromises.

So, if even the experts have resigned themselves to the fact that some men don't want to commit, then what can you do about it? Are you destined to a lifetime of being scared to call him your boyfriend in case he freaks out and emigrates? Will you forever be wondering if he's out talking to his mates about how much he likes you, or talking to some other girl about how much he likes her? Why can't you get him to commit to anything deeper than Friday-night football with the boys?

The answer is that being part of a couple has never really been marketed very well to boys. Us girls have been flashed beautiful images of wonderful houses, amazing pets and cute children, and promised that all this could be ours if we could just tie down a man. Any man. And the men? What marketing tactics have they been subjected to? Well, think James Bond, page 3 and swanky bachelor pads. In short, certainly from a social theory point of view, men have just been socialised to see commitment completely differently to women. To an extent, many women still see commitment, children and marriage as the ultimate goal, whereas many men see these things as a curtailment of freedom.

So how on earth do you fight against years of social and evolutionary conditioning? If he sees commitment as a pain in the backside, can you really make him see things differently? You're sick of him refusing to hold your hand in public, tired of his insistence that he could 'still pull if he wanted to' and growing bored of his romantic claims that he 'quite likes you'. But it's a tricky situation. Because if you're dealing with a commitment-phobe, screaming, crying and sobbing about how he just doesn't love you enough won't help. In fact, the only person it will help is whoever owns the airline he uses to escape the country. Any moves that suggest you are trying to manipulate him into commitment will only make him dig his heels in and feel even worse about tying himself to you. So make him see that commitment isn't all about loss.

Here's what to do about it

In fact, you have the power to completely resell commitment to him. Imagine all that rubbish marketing hasn't been done for years and years, and take a new stance. Repackage commitment. Make it your project. If he's your target market how are you going to get him hooked? Well, for a start, you need to make commitment sound exciting. Nagging that he can't go out because he needs to save so that you two can get a mortgage won't work. But getting excited and talking about how cool it would be if you pooled your money because then you can look for a house that's big enough to house his brand new snooker table, and throwing in magic phrases like 'snooker room', 'boys' nights in' and 'unlimited beer', will definitely be a step in the right direction. Or how about this one. Don't moan that he wants to spend too much time with the boys. Tell him that this weekend you're going out with the girls, and you don't want to see him all night so he should probably see the boys, but you want to sleep at the same place as him after – yours or his – so you can snuggle up and have a good gossip about the evening. Let him see that he can have the best of both worlds, and try to resell commitment so it doesn't seem like a trap.

That doesn't mean you shouldn't be aware of his fears. Talk to him. It's easy to assume that he's terrified that you're going to propose, or want babies straightaway, or to keep him under lock and key if he gets more serious with you. You need to discuss his fears with him, because the reality is that he might just be scared about his weekly pint down the pub being abolished. Or you forcing him to traipse around the shops every Saturday instead of letting him play a round at his favourite golf course. If his concerns are this straightforward, then they're pretty easy to relieve. Tell him that all of the things he loves doing are safe. Commitment to you doesn't mean a lifestyle change, it doesn't mean something borrowed, something blue. It just means a little awareness that there is a mutual respect and aspect of reliability in your relationship that perhaps wasn't there before. You're not going to chain him up and ban his rowdy, fun friends from coming round – at least until that new carpet has been fitted . . .

The good news is that most men are, in fact, 'the marrying kind' – most men are keen to get married at some point. However, they are just waiting longer and longer to actually do it. So don't despair, getting him down that aisle might just be a little bit like getting him to finally shave that beard, fix that leak or wash that car. He'll sulk and drag his heels, but you'll get him there in the end . . .

QUICK TIPS

1. Hide the bridal magazines.
2. Plan a few raucous nights out with your girls. It'll help remind him that you have a fun, carefree life you want to hold on to too.
3. Don't call him 'bunnykins' in front of his friends. He'll feel like he's just had his testicles publicly removed.

Q. My new boyfriend may be cooling off. Help!

Here's what's happening and why

At the beginning it's all hearts and roses. Like love's young dream, you truly are on cloud nine, in your own little world – and just about every other love cliché you can imagine. When you're not making each other laugh, going on great dates or having fantastic sex, you spend your hours thinking about how wonderful he is. Your mum's Celine Dion album takes on a new meaning as you begin to realise that, in fact, Celine had it right all along. You too believe in the 'Power of Love' and you too know that the 'Heart Will Go On'. And you can't even remember what's going on in your friend's lives, in fact you're pushed to remember their first names. And, although you are of course maintaining your air of laid-back nonchalance, secretly you're making plans for the obviously impending nuptials. You just can't decide on a spring wedding or a holly-decked church in November. Decisions, decisions . . .

But then, suddenly, something just doesn't seem right. It just doesn't feel the same. The phonecalls-per-day count drops from three hundred to just twenty. He's less complimentary when you turn up round his for an evening in. Admittedly, you're wearing your baggiest tracksuit bottoms and skankiest t-shirt, but he always used to think you looked 'so cute' in your sloppy clothes. He doesn't look at you in the same way. It just feels different and you don't know why. It's very easy to assume that the love of your life is about to turn into the love disaster of your life. It's understandable if you feel that the object of your affections has lost interest a little. But before you write off the relationship and begin your six-month man-mourning period, take a little time to examine the situation.

Well, firstly you need to be realistic. The excitement, the uncertainty and the butterflies in your tummy that accompany the first stages of a relationship are lovely, but they don't last forever. They can't. National telephone poles would melt and we'd be facing a global tree crisis to provide for the millions and trillions of Just-because-I-love-you cards needed. You can't find out what your boyfriend's favourite colour is for the rest of your life. There's only so many times you can hold hands for the first time. And eventually you have to let him know the truth about what you really sleep in. (Sorry darling, the lacy negligee may have been a bit misleading, but my Winnie-the-Pooh t-shirt is very sexy too . . .) So before you begin to panic that your relationship is heading for the scrapheap, ask yourself if the change is really a crisis or just a natural progression.

Research shows that however passionate relationships are to begin with, they will eventually hit a cooling-off period where they reach a more platonic stage. Now, that's not to say that you're going to start sleeping in different rooms and start calling each other 'mate'. It just means that you may not feel the same type of intensely lustful moments with quite the same frequency. And this stage has many plus points. For one, it means that you are free to relax a little. You don't have to wake up twenty minutes before he does to apply a full face of make-up. You don't have to panic when he says he can't make dinner because of work, because you know that he really does have work. You can let him know a few of your little secrets, like how many mars bars you can eat in one sitting, and your previously undisclosed ambition to enter *Pop Idol*. Because once you pass the 'first flushes' stage, you can relax a little, safe in the knowledge that you have more of a commitment from him. Enjoy it.

Also, this stage means that you can find out more about him. OK, so you know exactly who'd play in goal for his all-time football dream team and what he calls his car, but do you really know about his beliefs, principles, desires and fears? 'Tell me about your deepest fear' might not make great first-date conversation material, but once you pass the trivial chitchat stage you can probe a little deeper. And it can be more rewarding than knowing exactly what boxer shorts he prefers. Just like you will feel more secure after a certain amount of time, so will he, and this is when you can really get to know him. Far from being a sign of imminent collapse, a slight cooling off can be just what your relationship needs to move on to the next level.

Here's what to do about it

However, if you sense that the cooling off is a little more than a normal progression, or if it occurs very soon in the relationship, then it could be a sign that all is not well. And if you're unhappy then you really should address the problem. Be realistic, one tense phone call doesn't mean that he's gone off you. He could be having a bad day at work, perhaps he's stuck in a traffic jam, maybe his team's just been relegated. It doesn't mean he's going to relegate you. So don't take any sudden action. If the pattern continues for more than about a week, then this could be time to confront him with your feelings.

And once you've established that something in the relationship has definitely changed for the worse, then confrontation really is the only solution. If you're scared that he really has lost interest, then it can seem easier to avoid the talk in case he actually confirms all your fears. But burying your head won't make the situation go away, and if he has decided you're not 'the one', then it won't change his mind. If you ignore the issue for too long, you'll set a precedent where you feel neglected but you're too scared to establish whether you're being highly perceptive or just highly paranoid. If he has lost interest, then it really is best to discover that as soon as possible so that you can move on and save on wasted time in a relationship that's not going anywhere. Think about it logically, if you ask him how he feels you'll receive one of two answers. He'll either be shocked by your concern and act to calm any fears you may have. He'll probably have a feasible explanation for the cooling off and, as mentioned before, it'll probably feature work or football. Or the other outcome is that you'll discover that actually he's just not interested, in which case you can move on without trundling on completely oblivious to how he's feeling.

And if the cooling off is a genuine loss of interest, then try not to internalise the rejection too much. Yes, you may have been more into the relationship than he was, but it doesn't make you a failure. Perhaps he's just looking for something a little different. Maybe he's not ready to settle down. Maybe he feels you're not ready for the commitment. At least his honesty means that you are free to move on the next!

QUICK TIPS

1. Do not misinterpret him sulking about the football results as a sign that your relationship is heading down the pan.
2. Do not drone on incessantly about how your relationship is going stale. Because then it will.
3. If the downturn becomes too dramatic, be direct and confront it.

Q. Why is he so cagey when I try to talk about past relationships?

Here's what's happening and why

There is a line in *Sex and The City* where Samantha tells Carrie, 'Honey, you look back so much you should have a relationship rear-view mirror.' And the fact is that our dearly-departed Carrie is not the only woman who refers back to her relationship scrapbook every now and then. In fact, most of us could do with a relationship rear-view mirror. It takes us six months to snag the man we've been lusting after, three months to figure out that actually he's not the one, and three decades to stop talking about it. If you overhear a woman talking to her friends about her man troubles, undoubtedly they'll all pipe up with similar tales of male-related woe: 'Oh, that's just like Jason', 'Oh, you and Mark are so like me and Rob, all over again!' or 'I think the reason that me and Paul aren't working out is because of what happened between me and Joe.' It's like we keep an emotional diary of every romantic experience we go through. And when we meet new men, we're more than willing to let him know exactly where we're coming from, who hurt us, who didn't, what worked out, what didn't etc., etc. So it's only fair that he reciprocates, right?

So why does he reach for the remote control every time you bring up his exes, and mumble something about missing *Stars in Their Eyes* (which you know he hates)? How come every time you ask him what his last girlfriend was like, he stutters, 'Erm . . . OK', then changes the subject? If you're so willing to share why can't he open up a bit more? Is it because he doesn't trust you? Is it because he doesn't like you enough? Or perhaps he has a dark, dangerous closet full of skeletons? Maybe his ex was an international supermodel. Maybe his ex was a man. Maybe he used to be a woman. And so your imagination runs wild, fuelled by his lack of enlightenment. Before you asked what his ex looked like, you weren't really that bothered, until he completely avoided the question and started talking about football. Now, the question consumes your daily routine, as you sneakily search his room for clues and interrogate his parents. When you buy a car, you expect a full service history, so if you're planning on making a major investment in him, why can't he provide you with his service history?

There are probably two reasons for his reluctance to fill you in on every girlfriend he's ever had. The first is another one of those monumental differences between men and women. He just doesn't understand the point. He went out with a girl, it didn't work out, they broke up. What's the big deal? It's finished, over, completed. So why the hell do you keep banging on about it? Men are far more forward-focused on women, and they tend to spend less time dwelling in the past. To him, the most important thing is what's happening in the here and now, not who either of you went out with ten years ago. And when you think about it, it's rather healthy really. Because while you're trawling through the archives of past relationships, trying to explain parts of the present, he's just getting on with the present. It could be you that misses out in the end. Also, men tend not to associate the same emotional import-ance to memories as women do. So the past really isn't as important to him as it is to you. It doesn't dictate the future, and it's finished with, so he probably can't see the point in constantly referring to it.

Secondly, men have sussed out what happens when they do decide to divulge the deepest parts of their life B.Y. (Before You). They're not stupid, and there's a lot of mileage in the saying 'Once bitten, twice shy.' Oh no, you won't catch him out this time. Because he hasn't forgotten, he still remembers what happened when he decided to tell his last girlfriend that the one before her was a really nice, attractive girl, who had a great career and a size eight figure. He signed himself up to weeks and eventually months of questions like 'Was she prettier than me?', 'Am I fatter than her?' and 'So who was better in bed?' Men suspect that the more information they give us, the more we will have to use research for a little obsessive com-parison. They've learnt that whatever answer they give is likely to be the wrong one, or at least not the right one, so it's safer to keep quiet. And you can't really blame them.

Here's what to do about it

But a little curiosity is natural, especially if he's being cagey. Also, learning things about a person that they don't feel comfortable divulging straightaway is part of a new relationship. So there are steps you can take to try and make him share more freely. For a start, if you want him to tell you about his past, then explain a bit more about yours. Don't say, 'Well, John my ex used to make me scream so loud, I woke the neighbours!' He does not, repeat, does not want to hear about you having sex with another man. In fact, it's pretty much a surefire kiss of death to his confidence, his desire to share and probably the relationship in general. But you could say, 'I'm sorry if you feel I don't call enough during the day. My last boyfriend wasn't really so keen to talk to me all the time, so it's something I need to adapt to. Have you always spoken to girlfriends a lot during the day?' That way, he won't feel like he is undergoing the Spanish Inquisition, and the conversation will feel more natural.

Also, it will help if you can give him a rational explanation for why you want to know about his past relationships. So asking about what bra size his ex was, or how her lasagne tasted won't go down well. But explaining that you've noticed he's previously always gone for career women, and asking him whether it bothers him that you're not quite so career focused, is fair. Be specific, and reasonable. If he can understand where you're coming from then he's far more likely to give you a straight answer. He won't feel like he's being interrogated, and you'll be more satisfied with his answer.

Don't go into it like a madwoman possessed. If he really feels uncomfortable sharing with you then respect his privacy. If he has been scarred by a previous relationship, digging into the deepest recesses of his sorrow with you might not be his idea of a fun night in. So leave it. If he insisted you tell him, detail by detail, about every rejection or humiliation you've ever received, you'd probably feel a bit uncomfortable. And be realistic, you can't expect him to sit down in one session and help you compile lists of names, addresses and national security numbers. Over time, parts of his past will arise and you can deal with them then. Don't demand everything at once, give it time and he'll open up more and more.

QUICK TIPS

1. Don't hand him a questionnaire to fill in about every girl he's ever been out with.
2. Don't make the mistake of assuming he wants to hear you give past boyfriends marks out of ten for their bedroom abilities.
3. Be honest with yourself about why you care so much about his past.

Q. He's still best friends with his ex. Should I be bothered and what do I do if I am?

Here's what's happening and why

It can be hard to understand how your boyfriend can be

such good friends with his ex, especially if all of your exes have been filed under 'Dead to me'. How can they be 'just friends' if they've seen each other naked? Why isn't he attracted to her, after all she's beautiful and they did fancy each other once? And what do they really get up to on their secret lunch dates?

The fact is, when we form new relationships, there are aspects of our life that we have to reveal and share, because if they are important to us then it is important to the significant other that they are aware of them. So, you've introduced him to your favourite teddy bears, your gaggle of girly friends and your slightly scary mother. You thought it was all going swimmingly as he introduced you to Bertie, his clapped-out old beetle convertible, his dishy older brother and his collection of football memorabilia. Until he wheeled out Abbie, his infuriatingly gorgeous friend. Well, you thought she was a friend anyway. They do lunch. He helps her when her car breaks down. And she knows his family really well. So you can't help but wonder. So one day you ask, 'So, have you and Abbie ever snogged or anything?' He shrugs half-heartedly and drops the bomb-shell that changes everything. 'Yeah, we used to go out.' Your brain shatters, your imagination flips in circles and you coolly volunteer (hoping he won't notice the steam coming from your ears and the tinge of green developing in your eyes), 'Oh cool. How long did you go out for?' 'Oh, about three years or something, not sure.' Three years? Three years?!!

Although the history between him and his ex might not mean anything to him, if it matters to you then you need to say something. And you need to get it straight from the start, because the longer you leave it, the longer you have to build a non-issue into a relationship-threatening crisis. You don't have to go in guns ablazing and demand that he produces a written history of him and his ex-girlfriend. Try something like, 'It's nice that you and [you fill in the gap] can still be friends. What happened between you two?' He'll probably come up with a perfectly satisfactory answer. For most people, staying friends with an ex is not about secret desires to re-kindle the passion they once shared. It can make things easier if there are mutual friends involved. Perhaps there is a wish to stay in touch with the family. Perhaps it's about familiarity. Sometimes the 'friends with the ex' thing just springs from a sense of loyalty, or a sense of duty to what is the right thing to do when a break-up occurs. Nine times out of ten, the one thing that staying friends with an ex is not about is getting back together. Because, let's face it, if you and an ex still had feelings for each other, you wouldn't masquerade as best friends, you'd just get back together. So don't be afraid of their friendship. If you sense that the relationship is perfectly innocent, and everyone involved knows exactly where they stand, then there really is nothing to be worried about.

Here's what to do about it

If, however, you do feel uncomfortable with some aspect of the friendship, then you're going to have to refer back to those good old boundaries we keep talking about. Be aware of what you find acceptable and what makes you feel uncomfortable, and let him know. Be clear and rational, and give him a full explanation. So don't say, 'I hate it when you and Belinda see each other, stop it now.' Instead, be more specific and more explanatory, so say, 'I feel a little left out when you and Belinda go out for lunch, which makes me feel insecure, so that's why I get a little defensive.' If you are clear and fair, then he really should make every effort to allay your concerns. Ask him to talk you through exactly what him and his ex get up to when they meet. Where do they go? What do they talk about? Ask if next time they get together you can pick him up or drop him off, and then he can introduce the two of you. People can seem far more threatening to your relationship before you meet them, because it allows you to build all sorts of fantasies in your head about wild, flirty nights in romantic restaurants and cosy kissing on country picnics. It allows you to picture her as Angelina Jolie's sexier, more charismatic twin sister. Meeting the reality rubbishes these fantasies and helps you to know exactly what you're dealing with. If she has a partner too, why don't you suggest a double date? If he really values his friendship with his ex and his relationship with you, he'll appreciate your efforts to get to know her. Don't gate-crash every time they arrange to meet, but let him know that you're keen to get to know her.

If you're honest and reasonable, the ex-question can be fairly easily dealt with. However, there is one cardinal sin when it comes to his friendship with the lady before you. Never, ever, ever forbid him to see her. Although the idea of prohibiting any contact might sound like an appealing one, by issuing a 'me or her' ultimatum you put yourself in an impossible position. At first glance it might sound like a proactive, girl-power way of grabbing the problem by the neck and dealing with it. You don't like him spending time with her, so ban it, right? No. No. No. For two reasons. Firstly, if he doesn't agree, or worse, agrees and then disobeys you, you may never get over it. If you force him to cease contact with his ex, you put him in a position where he has to sever a friendship he values, or he'll just carry on seeing her in stealth mode. So, he'll be making secret plans, and you'll find yourself checking pockets and credit-card statements, or thumbing the *Yellow Pages* for the number of a private detective to follow him. And the second consequence is that he'll actually agree to your friendship veto and cut ties with his ex. The worst possible result is him ditching his friend. 'Brilliant,' you think, 'now that poisonous bitch is off the scene, me and my wonderful boyfriend can live happily ever after.' Great – if you want to live happily ever after with a gutless loser who displays an appalling lack of loyalty to his friends. Him forgoing his friendship is not the perfect solution. Understanding your insecurities, where they come from and how to deal with them, is.

QUICK TIPS

1. Never take your feelings of jealousy out on his ex-girl-friend. It's not her fault.
2. Don't play games, be honest.
3. Don't try and change his mind about his friendship with his ex by convincing him she is fatter, uglier or nastier than you. It won't work.

Q. How do I judge the pace at which the relationship should be moving?

Here's what's happening and why

You know how annoying it is when you ask somebody a question and their reply is, 'Well, that's a difficult one, how long's a piece of string?' Well, unfortunately, that really is the type of answer that's required for this question. Infuriating, but true. Every relationship in the world is completely different, and you won't find the answer to questions like this in *The Universal Guide to Relationships*. (That's largely because it doesn't exist, but you get the point.) While some of us race into relationships at a pace that rivals the world land-speed record, others prefer to ease themselves into being a couple. (You know, the ones who are still living in separate houses after four years, then get engaged ten years later, then marry a further twenty years along the line.) Each relationship depends on the man, it depends on the woman and it depends on the combination between the two. So don't ever feel that the pace you're moving at is 'wrong', unless you're unhappy. If you are unhappy, then there are a few moves you can make to gauge the speed of things and then make sure it is a speed you are happy with.

Here's what to do about it

You can learn to judge the perfect pace through each other. So learn to pick up on signs from him, and give him little signs that he can work from. If he wants you to meet his family after two dates, it might seem a little scary, but at least you know how he's looking at things. If you're not ready for it, then politely make excuses and wait until you are. Equally, if after three years you still don't know if his family actually exist, then you'll probably feel that the relationship is moving a little slowly. A lot of this, of course, will depend on whether you've found a man who's desperate to settle down, or a complete commitment-phobe.

Don't feel that you have to wait for him to dictate the speed of things. If he still hasn't asked you round for Sunday lunch at his parents and you feel ready for that step, then why not ask him if he wants to meet your family? Don't make a big deal out of it, don't begin with 'I know I'm asking a lot, and I'll understand if you're not ready, but . . .', just mention that you head back home every Sunday and it would be nice if he could join you. He'll only think it's a big, scary issue if you make it sound like one. He might have been dying to ask you to meet the folks, but concerned that you would think he was too keen, so he held back. By making the first move you give him permission to do the same, and when you come to the next step he'll feel more confident making the initial approach.

Likewise, if you're still unsure whether or not you're allowed to call him your boyfriend yet, then there's nothing stopping you making the first move. A very confusing limbo period can occur when you're not quite sure whether he's 'a bloke you're seeing' or 'your boyfriend'. Asking seems so primary school, but assuming and consequently scaring the hell out of him doesn't bear thinking about. And you might not have to confront the issue when discussing him with people at work, after all he's never going to know if you're calling him your mate, your boyfriend or your husband is he? And, to an extent, you're OK when telling parents he's your boyfriend because, of course, just like in maths at school, you have to round up to the next clear answer. 'Seeing' or 'courting' is like a 0.75 between the 0 of being strangers and the 1 that is a full blown relationship. So rounding up to 1 and calling him your boyfriend is perfectly acceptable when explaining to the old folks, because everything in between is lost on them. But just wait until that first time you go to a party with him, and you go to introduce him to somebody. 'This is Tom, my . . . erm . . . splutter, choke, cough . . . erm, this is Tom.' Very smooth. You can avoid the embarrassment by having a quick two-minute chat with him about it. If it's easier, blame the need for clarification on somebody else: 'Sharon at work asked me if we were boyfriend and girlfriend today! What do you reckon . . . ?' Just like when he first lets you wear his favourite football shirt, or lets you drive his car for the first time, you can give him little pointers that will help him map out exactly where you want to be.

Don't be pressurised by anybody else. Who cares if your best friend met her man at the same time as you and they're moving in together? If you and your man are still happy at the sussing out which side of the bed you want to sleep on stage, then that's fine. There's no rule book. And let's face it, if there was you'd probably break all of the rules anyway wouldn't you . . . ?

QUICK TIPS

1. Matching tattoos after three weeks is *always* too hasty.
2. Introducing him to your parents is one thing. Expecting

him to spend the whole weekend fishing with your dad is quite another.

3. There is no such thing as a relationship speedometer. Just go with what feels best.

Q. He and my best friend hate each other. What can I do?

Here's what's happening and why

So you love your best friend. She's been through everything, good times, bad times, good shoes, bad hair. She's shared every important moment with you. She has a soggy shoulder from the number of times you've cried on it. And you couldn't imagine life without her. She's funny, kind, warm, supportive and reliable. Then there's your man. The one you thought would never come along. The one who's slowly but surely progressing from being an exciting novelty to being a permanent fixture. He's funny, kind, warm, supportive and reliable too. So why the hell do they hate each other so much? Your fantasy of a beautiful wedding day where your wonderful bridesmaid follows you up the aisle to your wonderful husband is slowly ruined by more colourful, and frankly more likely, images of the bridesmaid screeching up the aisle ten yards ahead of you to kick ten shades of hell out of your beloved, just before executing the perfect speech she has prepared in response to the minister's request for any reason why you and him shouldn't tie the knot. Great. So what do you do? On the one hand you owe her the loyalty that years of friendship demands. Equally, you owe him the same support that he has shown you. So whose word do you take? Is she really a scheming, jealous cow? Is he really a lying, cheating waste of space? Who do you listen to?

Here's what to do about it

Neither of them. That's the only answer. If both your friend and your man are massively important to you, then you need to make it clear that you are sitting firmly on the fence (regardless of how many splinters your backside receives!). You also need to make it clear that you also expect a certain amount of maturity from both parties, purely to make life easier for you. Whatever their feelings about one another, both need to remember that their loyalties are to you, and they should try to ease the tension. Often these situations can be about territory. Perhaps your friend is used to you having more time for her and feels that you have been taken away by your boyfriend. Maybe she has just come out of a relationship and she wants more time from you, and feels she deserves it because you are such good friends. Maybe your boyfriend feels that your newly-single friend poses a threat to your relationship, because she'll take you on raucous nights out and lead you astray. Neither he nor her owns you, so be clear about that. They can't fight over you like two toddlers and a skipping rope.

The worst thing you can do with a dispute like this is pay it too much attention. Don't sit down and demand crisis talks about who knew you first and who owns the most rights to your time. Because then you just give the argument credibility. Simply refuse to be a part of the argument. If she comes to you with a whole batch of colourful new insults she's acquired to bad-mouth him, then tell her you're not interested. Likewise, if he wants to talk about how much weight she's put on recently, tell him you don't want to hear it. Bitching becomes very boring if nobody's listening to you. Simply refuse to indulge their childish banter. And make them both fully aware that you are refusing to get involved. Because he's probably worrying that she is 'poisoning' your thoughts with awful lies about him, and she may well be worrying that when she's not there he's 'turning you against her'. So make it clear that bitching is off bounds, then everybody knows what the game rules are.

And remember, there's no reason that you can't maintain successful relationships with both parties, even if they hate each other. Remind them that if they care so much about you, they should show respect for the things that mean the most to you. So, although him indoors might not be a massive fan of your best girly mate, he needs to appreciate that she has been a good friend to you, and he should respect her for always being there for you. In fact rather than swiping and scratching, he should be thanking your best mate for looking after you. Likewise, if you truly have found happiness in this new man, then your friend should be happy for you and at least try to understand what it is about him that you're so fond of. They don't have to like each other for the sake of each other, but they do have to be respectful for your sake. It's a real shame if your boyfriend and your best friend can't get on, but it's not the end of the world. Just see them separately, as long as they both agree that you won't listen to negative criticism of the 'enemy'. Ask them to be polite to one another when they are forced to see each other, for example at your birthday party, for your sake. Explain that it is important to you that you can spend special days with both of them.

And leaving them alone for a while might sound about as stupid as leaving a cat and a dog together for half an hour, but it might actually have a real impact on their relationship. If the point of contention between them is you, then take yourself out of the equation. If you're always there, then you'll form an anchor for conversations and only serve to emphasise the fact that you are their only link. Suggest that him and her spend some time together, just the two of them, and they'll probably find that they have a number of things in common besides you. If they survive the day without kicking, biting or scratching, they might just end up as friends, so surely it's worth a try?

QUICK TIPS

1. Do not, repeat, *do not* get involved.
2. Never agree with one when they are moaning about the other, you'll just be giving them a licence to bitch.
3. Don't expect them to be best chums, but make it clear that you expect them to be civil.

Q. He's crowding me! How do I tell him that I like him, but I need my space?

Here's what's happening and why

You like him. You really do. He's the type of guy you never thought you'd find – he's got a brain for a start. And you're pretty sure that he likes you too. In fact you know he likes you. A lot. The twenty red roses you're currently receiving on a daily basis are a bit of a giveaway. And the fact that he's calling your mother 'Mum' must be a sign. And now when he talks about going out with his mates, he means your mates. And he's always there: when you get home from work, when you wake up in the morning, when you get a coffee break, when you stay in, when you go out. And it is sweet, it's lovely. Your friends are envious, your mum can't help but shed a little tear when you mention his name because he's 'just so lovely' and even your cat has warmed to him. But if you're truly honest with yourself, you're not sure exactly how you feel about the whole palaver. Because you can't help but long for the days when you had 'you time' rather than 'us time', and when staying in and slobbing out meant you and a tub of Häagen-Dazs, not you and your clingy boyfriend. You can't help but wish that you had your double bed back to yourself every now and then. And you feel awful that you wish it was you telling that cute guy in the bar that you're not interested, not your lovable new sidekick. But how do you tell him? Because as much as you need a little independence, you don't want to lose him. And are you just being ungrateful? After all, you've spent years bemoaning the lack of men who are actually willing to commit.

Here's what to do about it

The answer is that if you like him and you truly respect him, you owe it to him to be honest. For the relationship to go any further, you need to tell him how you feel and what you need. Pre-empt a situation where you finally crack under the pressure and scream, 'Give me some space! I'm suffocated, you stalker!' Take control before the situation gets to that point, and be more sensitive. For example, you might feel 'suffocated', but that really isn't the word you should use because it only has negative connotations. If he's putting in all this effort and he feels like you are putting him down, then he may well back off. And not for a couple of days, but to the extent where you're longing for him to move back in and sing love songs to you all day, just like the old days.

So explain that you are really enjoying things and you are really into him, but you feel that perhaps this has started to get in the way of other priorities in your life. Perhaps you feel that you should spend a bit more time with your family so you can catch up on what you've missed and tell them all about your great new man. Maybe you're annoyed that you've begun to neglect work and you want to get back on track. Tell him that your friends have begun to notice that you're not calling them as much and you want to do a few lunch dates with them to make it up to them. Try and make it more about yourself than about him. Don't say, 'It's so annoying when you turn up just as I'm about to have a night in with me and my *Friends* box set.' Say, 'I'm sorry, I really feel like just being a real lazy, grouchy slob tonight, but can we do something tomorrow instead?' Don't make it feel like a personal criticism of his behaviour if you really like him.

Just give him a gentle reminder of what your boundaries are. Yes, he is a major priority in your life, but there are others and you're finding it tough to balance them all. If he's as interested as he's making out, then he'll care enough to want to make your life a little easier. Also, make it clear that giving each other some space can have benefits for him too. Don't say, 'This Saturday I want to go to see my mum and I don't want you there using every conversation to impress her.' Say, 'Mum wants me to pop over on Saturday, I thought it would be a great chance for you to play golf with the boys – you haven't seen much of them lately.' Or tell him that when you see each other you want it to be more about quality, not quantity, 'I'm going to be really busy and stressed out with work this week, so why don't we make Friday night a special evening for just you and me?'

And make sure you give him the same space back. When he adapts to fit your feelings, don't throw a tantrum when he isn't free on your day off. The strongest relationship is one where you are both free to fulfil all your commitments, including those that don't include each other.

QUICK TIPS

1. Be sensitive, this probably isn't his fault.
2. When confronting the situation with him, try to avoid using words like 'obsessive', 'trapped' or 'restraining order'.
3. Speak to him before you get a restraining order. Always.

MOVING ON . . .

The letters received about those first few weeks, or even months, of a new relationship all had one thing in common. Whether they discussed his hatred for your mother, or his 100 miles-per-hour rush to get you into bed, all of the problems presented issues of discovery. Discovery about yourself. Discovery about him. Discovery about what you will and will not accept. Discovery about the type of relationship you want. Discovery about how realistic these expectations are.

So really, the best way to approach relationship is to make like Christopher Columbus and don your very best 'discovery' hat. If you can't find one, a cute little sun visor or a funky fedora will do. In fact, forget the hat, it doesn't matter. What's important is that you do approach the discovery in the right way. Go into it boldly. That means knowing what you want. Don't expect anybody else to outline what you should want from a relationship – know it within yourself. Equally, don't let anyone else dictate what behaviour you find acceptable.

So this might mean that you need to do a little self-discovery before you get into a relationship with somebody else. Know yourself, because once you do you're in the best position to get to know somebody else. Know what your boundaries are and be prepared to learn that if he isn't comfortable with them then perhaps he isn't the right one for you. This makes it all the more special when you find somebody whose boundaries fit nicely with yours.

Be strong, be direct, be honest and you'll lay the best foundations you can for your potential relationship. And the next bit will be easy won't it? Well, no. But at least you will have established a firm set of principles that you both respect. This will help you move seamlessly into stage two. This is the stage when you aren't so much worrying about first dates and introducing him to your mother. Instead you row about spending seven nights a week watching TV in his flat, or the amount of time he spends with his boys down the pub. So at least you've got something to look forward to then . . .

Part Two

THE MIDDLE

TIME TO GET COMFY,
BUT NOT TOO COMFY . . .

Relationships are like shoes. You spot a brand-new pair of pink strappies that you just *know* will change your life. You long for them, you lust after them. You wrestle with your conscience and your credit card in the store, weighing up the financial costs against the obvious lifetime benefits. Yes, they may cost the price of a deposit on a small two-bedroom apartment, but clearly they will make you more beautiful, more desirable and happier. So, you make the investment. And only time can tell how wise it was. Because sometimes you get home and realise that, actually, you can't even walk in them. But every now and then you find a cracking pair that are really worth the longing, the lusting, the first-night blisters. They feel nice. And they're secure. You can walk, stand, run and perform drunken cartwheels, if necessary, without fear of losing your balance. They feel safe. And what's more, you still love, love, love them. Perfect. They might not last forever, but they have certainly secured their place in your all-time top ten, favourite shoes.

So you may well be grasping for the link between a

slinky pair of stilettos and your relationship, but there is one. Because like your relationship with a pair of shoes, your relationship with your man faces a few definite stages. First, there is the initial sighting. The immediate lust. The 'have to have you' feeling. Then there is the choice of how far forward you take that. Do you snap him up straight-away or do you take a closer look at the buckle, the straps and decide he's not quite what you were looking for? Then once you've made the investment, there is the honeymoon stage. You want to show off your new 'purchase', you are consumed with pride and you keep getting little butter-flies in your tummy. And then after that?

Well, the initial excitement wears off. It has to or you'd be in a state of permanent excitement for the rest of your life and, frankly, that's not helpful to anybody. But it changes to something new. You love your man for different reasons. Not just because he looks good in a suit and always gets the drinks in (although you do still love those things about him, of course), but also because he understands you, and he makes you feel safe and secure. Just like the shoes, you pass a point and it becomes comfortable instead of just lust-filled and frenetic.

But comfy and contented as this stage is, it does not come without it's problems. Just as the first few weeks might present you with issues related to finding the right man, letting him know and facing demons such as the 'first date', the months that follow can throw up problems related to commitment, coupling and retaining your own individuality. Ladies, read on, if you will . . .

LAY SOLID FOUNDATIONS

If the first few weeks are about setting boundaries, the next stage is about living with them. Imagine, if you will, that building a relationship is like building a home (well, at least we've moved off the shoe analogy!). In the first few weeks, you're digging holes and laying foundations, setting boundaries and establishing exactly where you want your walls to be. You have to do all these things before you actually move in, and that's the stage that we're at now. So if you've established who you are and who you will be within the relationship, this is the part where you actually get to be that person. So you might have used the first few weeks to establish to him that you need your own space and you don't want to spend every single night with him. This is when you begin to live with that 'rule'. And this is where you begin to establish the rhythm of the relationship, which will play an integral part in helping both of you to establish exactly what to expect from each other individually, and what you can expect as a couple.

So, in those first stages you're both groping around in the dark, trying to establish how often you are going to see each other, how often you are going to argue, how often you are going to spend time with your friends and how often you are going to, well, grope around in the dark. So you still wonder if your reply to his email is just a little too speedy. Or if wanting to see him for the third night in a row is just a little bit too stalker-ish. And you lay awake, panicking, the first time you spend the night together and he wants to *sleep* with you in the word's most basic sense. Or you fall out over him turning up forty-five minutes late to pick you up, and you spend the rest of the day wailing to your friends over your deep, dark fears that 'It's *over*!'

Oh yes, the beginnings of relationships are uncertain times, because nobody really knows what is expected of them and what they should be expecting in return. But as you encounter each new experience as a couple, that first sleepover, that first family occasion, that first row in a supermarket, slowly, and unwittingly, you are establishing precedents and setting boundaries.

By the time we move into the middle stage of the relationship, we have established this rhythm. We know how often to expect romantic gestures, sex, big nights out and little unnecessary 'I love you's', whether that is not very often or all the time. This rhythm is important because you both know where you stand. But it is also useful because it helps you to differentiate between when things are trundling along just swimmingly, and when things are not quite as hunky-dory as they should be. So if you've gone from expecting a massive row once every month, to suddenly finding yourself enduring World War-style engagement every night, then the fact that your rhythm has been disturbed should give you a little hint that things aren't going as well as they have in the past. That's if the smashed crockery, broken furniture and slammed doors don't give you a tip off . . .

The fact is that establishing a rhythm allows us to monitor, more clearly, exactly how the relationship is progressing. It gives us a benchmark. If you're used to seeing him three times a week and suddenly he wants to see you every other weekend, it sets alarm bells ringing. If you're used to him ringing you at work four times a day to tell you that he thinks you're beautiful and then it suddenly stops, it can be a little disconcerting. The middle stage is often about what happens when your rhythm goes through changes, and how you deal with that. One less phonecall a day does not necessarily mean your relationship is slowly sinking into that black hole every other relationship you've had seems to have disappeared down. It might just mean that you've settled into the next, less intense stage, and although your boundaries shouldn't change, you might need to adapt your expectations slightly.

RECOGNISE YOUR JOINT PERSONALITY

Another key characteristic of this stage in your relationship's development is the birth of your joint personality. Because you will find that your name no longer exists on its own. Your first name may soon be incapable of standing alone in a sentence. It'll happen gradually, and suddenly one day you'll wake up and realise that you are no longer Karen. You are 'KarenandSteve', or 'KarenandMark', or 'KarenandJon', or whatever your other half's name is. If you turn up at a wedding alone, people will want to know where he is (once they've established via method of hushed whispering that you haven't been dumped). If your name is on an invitation then you can bet your bottom dollar that his is too. And the same with your Christmas cards. You'll start to overhear your mother referring to you and him by your new collective name.

And the two of you, besides taking ownership of a new name, also, unsuspectingly, adopt a new personality. A joint personality. Think about your friends in relationships. There's probably the 'fun couple'. You know, the ones who you always invite if you're going out on the town, the ones who you have to drag home at four in the morning after she's terrorised every single barman and he's been thrown out for puking on his shoes. Then there is the 'grown-up couple', the ones who make you feel civilised and sophisticated because they go to lovely wine bars and always turn up with Harrods hampers when you go out for picnics in the park. Then there is the 'reliable couple', the ones who are always there to give lifts to the airport and walk the dog when you go away.

The longer you spend with someone, as you adjust to one another, the more your relationship develops a personality of its own. This originates from the way you relate to one another, the things you do together and the boundaries and foundations you have set for your relationship. So perhaps you're the 'funny couple', because you're always bantering and bickering light-heartedly with one another. Maybe you're the 'sporty couple', because you're always out in the park jogging or going to watch the football together. Or perhaps you like to think you're the 'perfect couple' because you never, ever row, and you always, always support one another, and you never, ever get cross with each other. No? Didn't think so. Don't worry, they don't actually exist . . .

And whatever your 'joint personality', you and your partner will also develop roles within your relationship. This is common within any group or unit. Think about team-building exercises at work, you know the ones: 'Work out a way to get this sack of corn past the imaginary farmer, without waking the chicken next to him, before sneaking back to steal his combine harvester – in teams of six. Go!' There's always somebody who is determined to be the most vocal and talk over everybody else, firmly asserting their position as leader. Then somebody will automatically slip into the role of the quiet thinker. Some people will quickly fade into the background, assuming the role of the followers. (Of course, some people will just sneak out for a fag and coffee because they couldn't care less if Farmer Jack loses a bag of corn, but that's besides the point . . .)

The fact is that the precedents and routines that you set in the first few stages of a relationship establish exactly what part you will play. So you might settle into roles where he is always the loud one and you tend to keep quiet until he's introduced you or brought you into the joke. Or maybe you're the outgoing one, and you tend to be a spokesperson for the two of you when you're at a restaurant, or at the mechanics, or at his parents, even. However, the most common role that women feel they slip into is the role of 'mother'. No one intends to find themselves picking up their boyfriend's socks and clearing up the mess he left after breakfast, but before they know it they've attended the audition, learnt the lines and got the part.

Partly due to evolution and the caring, organisational role that prehistoric women naturally assumed, women find it far easier to slip into this role. And social conditioning plays an important part here too. If you look at traditional female roles and compare them to traditional male roles, it's fairly obvious that women have been conditioned into thinking that organising and care-taking are their responsibilities. Think maids, secretaries and nurses. Think about wartime social structure when Britons were enrolled as soldiers or carers, depending entirely upon their gender. Because of years of belief that every good man has the backing of a strong woman who supports him, cares for him and gets those curry stains out of his favourite work tie, many women still feel that if their man can't look after himself, it's their responsibility to step in.

So you organise his dentist appointments. You tidy up after him. You make sure he's got clean shirts for work. You potty train him. Well, not quite. But sometimes it feels like that may well be the next step . . .

KEEP 'ME' SEPARATE FROM 'WE'

Now this is all well and good if you actually enjoy playing the roles that you appear to have acquired. Perhaps you are, by nature, a caring, organising person and you can think of no greater pleasure than sitting for six hours trying to pair up endless pairs of comedy cartoon-character socks so that he doesn't have to commit the heinous crime of wearing odd socks to the pub. Perhaps he enjoys being organised by you because if it was up to him, he'd never eat, wash, sleep or tidy up his stinking flat.

Roles like this can be great, because often they help us establish where we stand in a relationship and maximise the things we are both best at. But you should be aware of becoming trapped in these roles, especially if you are not happy playing them. Maybe you don't want to be his mother, maybe you want him to grow up a bit and assume a little independence and responsibility of his own. Maybe he's sick of you telling him what order to pack his suit-case in (why, oh why does it matter if the shoes *don't* go on the bottom and the towels *don't* go on the top?). There needs to be a degree of flexibility within these roles so that you can both be free to be who you want to be too.

So it sounds easy right? You work out what you're both good at, you let each other demonstrate these skills and work them into the effective functioning of your relationship. Oh, and you maintain an element of flexibility so if either of you feel a little trapped, there's room to manoeuvre. OK, so it doesn't sound that easy. It sounds rather complicated. So how do you achieve this harmonious state, this successful combination? Communication, a little bit of communication and, just for luck, some communication. The only way to figure out if you're both happy playing the roles you appear to have acquired is to talk about it. Don't assume he wants you to be his babysitter. Don't let him assume that you want him to make all the important decisions. Talk about it, and really get to know one another. The middle section of a relationship gives you the best opportunity to do this. So maximise the opportunity and make sure you don't end up playing Cinders when really you'd rather be living it up à la Prince Charming.

KNOWING ME, KNOWING YOU

OK, so at the beginning you might *think* you really know him. After all, you've talked about his favourite holiday destination, his favourite colour and his top five songs from the eighties. You know where he works, when he was born and what he drives. So surely you're fully armed with all you know to dive headfirst into a lifelong commitment to this man. If only he would just propose . . .

The middle stage is when you *really* get to know

somebody, at a far deeper level than what their favourite breakfast cereal is. You learn things like what his secret ambitions in life are, what he gets scared about, what he gets excited about. This is where you'll find out about that secret stamp collection, or his obsessive passion for train spotting. You've got past the part where you sit in quiet restaurants on dates, revealing little snippets of carefully selected information to each other. Think of those dates as being a bit like leafing through a holiday brochure. You know you're only getting told the best bits – ocean views, heated indoor pool, beautiful outdoor pool, luxury bedrooms, exquisite restaurant. The middle stage is the equivalent of boarding the plane, landing, arriving and really getting a chance to suss out just how accurate the brochure was. Now you might just find that the beautiful outdoor pool is more of a basin in a concrete yard, and the speciality of the house restaurant is 'Cockroach dans la soup'. But you may well find out that the reality is even better than you originally thought. With any luck, you'll find that the more you get to know your man, the more you like him.

As well as finding out more information for yourself, just through the time you spend with him, you will also find out more about his life through the other people you meet through him. Little sisters are always great comrades for pulling out the baby photos and, even more embarrassing, the teenage photos. OK, you know everyone had mullets, but why does his seem to look even more ridiculous than everybody else's? At least it gives you a chance to appreciate that, fortunately, Elton John is no longer his style icon.

Forming bonds with his friends and his family also allows you access to more information (without wanting to make your relationship sound too much like a government research project). Watching him with his mother, or with his mates down the pub, or with his little niece can tell you far more than he ever could about his relationships with others. This might also help you to understand him a little better. For example, if you do find that you have slipped into a mother-son type interaction, you might appreciate the reason for this once you've witnessed his mother greet him, unlace and remove his shoes, lead him to the dining table, sit him down, fetch him a napkin (which she then tucks into his collar), help him to some potatoes and them attempt to feed him. Your twenty-seven-year-old boyfriend. Suddenly, it all becomes clear . . .

But what if you don't feel that you are being allowed proper access to his history, his family and every skeleton in his closet? What if he isn't that keen on you meeting his parents, and what if he doesn't want to tell you the name, address and bra size of every girl he's ever been out with? Does this mean he's just not interested? Does this mean he's about to end it all? Well, probably not. In fact he's probably just displaying typical male reluctance to commit himself 100 per cent to the relationship at the same stage that you are ready to. Perhaps he feels that there are parts of his life that he's not ready to share with you yet. And that's fine. This stage doesn't mean that after confirming you are, in fact, a couple, your next step is to swap CVs, pull out birth certificates and pool bank accounts. It means that with time, gradually, you learn more and more about each other. And think about it this way, if he doesn't want you to attend his Stamp-mad Collectors' Club with him, then it's probably a good thing . . .

Basically, the middle stage is where you will acquire a greater depth of knowledge about your man, and it won't all necessarily come from him. It will come from friends, family and your own observations, and essentially it will form the basis of your decision to stay around or run for the hills. However, this should happen naturally and gradually, at a pace that ensures that you both feel you are keeping hold of your own identities within the framework of your relationship.

PACING IT

Think back to your school days, if you will. And remember Sports Day. You weren't selected for the glamorous relay team, you weren't selected for the glory of the 100 metre sprint, you weren't even considered competent enough for the egg and spoon race. All that was left was discus and the long distance events. So, proudly, (well, as proudly as you can in nylon shorts that keep rather inconveniently riding up your bottom) you stepped up and accepted the challenge that so many before you had shirked. You would bring the title home. You would put the glamour into the 400 metre. Oh yes you would. So as soon as you heard that gun (or that science teacher shout 'Go!'), you were off! Full speed, 100 miles per hour in your brand new plimsolls. Full throttle, revelling in the fact that everybody else seemed to be trailing a few metres behind. Glory would be yours! Never again would they laugh you out of the relay team, you'd be headhunted, possibly by the National Olympic Squad. But, hang on a minute, suddenly your opponents are catching up with you. And then they're not so much trailing behind you as ripping up the track ahead of you. And as you watch your school, national and possible international athletics career disappear in a puff of rubber plimsolls and cheap aertex t-shirts, all you can remember is your mum in the crowd, screaming with the manic force that only a proud pushy parent can muster, 'Pace it! Pace yourself! Pace it!' . . .

And that is a little bit what relationships are like. It can be really tempting to throw yourself hurtling at full throttle into a new relationship. During years as a single lady, it can often feel like the 'right man' is up with there with Father Christmas and the Tooth Fairy. So when, by some miracle, he does actually appear, our enthusiasm means it is easy to get carried away. So we want it all. And we want it now. We want to meet his family, we want to stay at his every night, we want to go out with his mates. However, flying full speed into all of these things can mean you run out of steam towards the end. Yes, in the beginning stage you should live for the moment and embrace each step wholeheartedly, but be wary that you aren't wanting too much too soon, and that you are allowing your relationship to develop at its own natural pace.

This middle stage is when you and him decide when you are ready to do all sorts of big 'coupley' things, from leaving a toothbrush at his house, to buying a house together. And there's no rule saying that you'll both be ready for the same steps at the same time, so it's important that you keep the lines of communication open so that either of you can press the pause button if you feel like things are running away with themselves, or if you're just feeling a little crowded.

Of course, the other thing that can happen is that you may well feel that the overall pace of your relationship has shifted down a gear. Perhaps you don't have the same mad urges to grope him in the supermarket. Maybe you don't call him six hundred times a day to tell him just how wonderful he is. Maybe you don't feel like you are lost in a crazy daze like you did in those first frantic stages of your relationship. And an important point to note here is that there are no rules dictating exactly how long these first stages should last. The 'honeymoon period' isn't called the 'honeymoon six months' or 'honeymoon two weeks'. It's indefinite. And it is different for every relationship. Perhaps life would be more simple if you could say, 'Right darling, we have been dating for four weeks and three days now, so according to the rules just four more days and it's time for you to meet my friends.' But it wouldn't be as much fun.

So maybe you feel like your relationship has changed. Maybe some of the initial excitement has died down. But this is because your romance has moved on to the next level. It would be impossible to remain in those first flushes of the honeymoon period forever. So your relationship settles and crystallises into something more solid, if a little less intense. This isn't necessarily a bad thing, in fact it is a very good sign that your relationship is progressing in a normal and natural way. However, some of its side-effects – a dip in sexual activity, a drop in excitement – can lead to problems that your relationship has never encountered before.

This second part deals with those problems, the problems that you just won't come across when you're still dating, flirting and sussing each other out. These are the issues that you encounter once you've accepted that you want to be in the relationship and you are ready to face the troubles that this may bring. From his ever-present ex to his seemingly non-existent family (they are to you, because he just won't let you meet them), the middle stage brings with it a fresh set of problems to be addressed. And if the first stage is about leafing through the brochure, this next stage is about working out whether the goods match the description . . .

Q. How come his friends seem more important than me?

Here's what's happening and why

They say you can judge a man by the company he keeps. And you're not quite sure what this says about your man, judging by the motley crew he likes to hang out with. It's not just that they all have nicknames that appear to derive from animals or strange versions of their surnames. It's not that they like to hang out at the smokiest, most un-hygienic pub in town. It's not even that they refer to you as 'battleaxe' and 'the boss', although that is mildly rankling. For you, the real problem is that, for all their obvious faults, they still appear to come top of his list of priorities. And you just can't understand it.

So, you've been planning his first meeting with your parents. It's all been arranged. They're expecting you and the new man at three o'clock sharpish. The tea cakes have been decanted onto the finest china plates. And you can't wait, because you're convinced that everyone's going to get on just swimmingly. Apart from it's now 2.45 and he's nowhere to be seen. His first audience with your parents could be a little pointless if he doesn't actually make an appearance. You try to keep calm. You know he's been playing rugby, maybe they went into extra time, maybe there was a problem with the car. He'll be home any minute. Well, that's what you tell yourself, although your predictions are all dashed when you call him and he can't string two words together. Because a swift half after the game has turned into eight. 'But Jonesy scored his first try for seven games!', he pleads as you remind him, with venom and fury, of his prior engagement. Yet again, he has chosen time with the boys over something that is important to you.

You know he cares about you, and you know he wants to be with you, but it can be hard to feel that you are as important to him as he is to you when Monday, Tuesday, Wednesday, Thursday, Friday and Saturday nights are reserved for time with the boys, and you are slotted in somewhere around Sunday evening. Likewise, when a wedding invitation drops through the door and he tactlessly announces that he'll take Macca as his guest because 'he loves a bit of free beer'. Or when your Mediterranean beach holiday fantasies are scuppered by the 18–30s brochures you keep seeing scattered on the coffee table. You're pretty sure that the 'ten nights in Ibiza for twelve people' that he keeps referring to on the phone to travel agents does not include you. You always think about him. He's the first number on your speed dial at work. You've put 'AAA' in front of his name in your mobile, so that he is the first contact in your phone book. When a big work function comes up, you've started to think about what you'll dress him in before you've even asked if partners are invited. And your friends have become used to seeing a little less of you, now that you have to make time for him too. You've adapted your life to make space for your new relationship, so why does it feel like he is just carrying on as he always has done? Why can't he make a few compromises for you?

Here's what to do about it

The problem is that to feel whole within a relationship, we also need to feel whole as an individual. And what we need to do to feel whole varies. You might feel comfortable cutting back a little on the amount you see your friends, but to him, seeing his friends might just be what makes him feel whole and content. A night down the pub with his friends might look fairly primitive to you, such is the swearing, shouting and boozing that goes on, but it might just be what he needs to make him feel grounded and secure. So you need to respect this and appreciate the things that are important to him.

Probably the worst thing you can do here is start making ultimatums and demands. Saying, 'It's your friends or me' is pretty much the kiss of death to any relationship. If he chooses the boys then you haven't really achieved the desired result. If he chooses you then he's displayed a worrying lack of loyalty to his friends. And it wouldn't make either of you happy. If this is an issue that you need to talk to him about, then don't say, 'You're not going to the pub tonight. If you leave this house, I'm leaving! After I've set light to your entire wardrobe!' Instead, explain that you really want to spend some more time with him and you need to feel that he is putting as much into the relationship. Don't blame his friends, in fact you don't even need to bring them into it, as this is likely to make him feel that his mates are being attacked, and will instantly pit you against him – and the men he loves. And also your feelings aren't really about his mates specifically, they're just about feeling important to him. So make the point that it's not his friends you have a problem with, it's the feeling of being second-best that really hurts.

Also, you can encourage him to behave in a certain way by behaving in that manner yourself. Show him that you are willing to adapt your schedule to fit him into your life. So when he says, 'Let's stay in and get pizza tonight,' say, 'Well, I had arranged to see Mum tonight, but if you really want to have a quiet night in, let's do that and I'll see her tomorrow.' Or let him know that you want to know when his days off are next week, so that perhaps you can try and plan some of your time off with him. Make it clear that you are happy to make changes for the relationship. If he can see that you are making compromises for him, he's far more likely to follow your lead.

And they do say, 'If you can't beat them, join them.' You might think his friends are a bunch of slobs/yuppies/animals [delete as appropriate], but if they're that important to him then perhaps you should get to know them a little bit better, and perhaps you'll see what all the fuss is about. If you are prepared to spend an evening down the pub with him and his friends, then he won't start seeing time with them and time with you as such mutually exclusive choices. Also, he'll appreciate the time you're giving up to be with him and show an interest in his interests. And who knows, you might actually have fun. Reeling off the current league positions, complete with goal differences and games in hand, could be a brilliant party trick. And everybody's impressed by the ability to down a pint in 0.6 seconds. Even if it's a pint of orange juice . . .

But make sure you know exactly what your fears are

here. Is he really prioritising his friends above you? Perhaps you're feeling insecure about something else within the relationship and this is manifesting itself through a need to be near him all the time. If approaching the problem in the ways mentioned above really doesn't help, then perhaps you need to do a little soul searching and discover the truth behind your feelings. Maybe you're unsure about what he gets up to when he is out with his friends and that is really what you're concerned about. Or perhaps your own insecurities are telling you that he has more fun with his friends and you are projecting these fears onto him? To get the best solution, you really need to be honest with yourself about what the actual problem is.

But if after all this you still feel that his priorities really lie elsewhere, then you need to refer back to those good old boundaries. If he isn't prepared to match you compromise for compromise, then will things ever change? After all, perhaps he feels that spending the majority of his leisure time with his friends and then rolling home to you at three in the morning is the perfect setup. Explain to him the difference between occasionally indulging in a little chocolate gateaux, and having your cake – and eating it. Every Saturday night. And, for that matter, every other night of the week. If your boundaries are being violated despite your repeat attempts to address the issue, then maybe you need to think about how seriously he sees this relationship. If you're just an added bonus at the end of another killer night out with the boys, then that might be all he will ever see you as. Trust your instincts – if you don't think things will ever change, and you're not happy with them, then get out now.

QUICK TIPS

1. Never make big scary ultimatums. Like, ever.
2. Don't attempt to dissuade him from spending time with his friends by slagging them off. Remember who he knew first.
3. If it's never going to change, then admit it and ask yourself if the situation will ever make you happy.

Q. Why doesn't he share my passion for shopping?

Here's what's happening and why

'Darling, wouldn't it be nice to go shopping together today? Let's take a trip up to town. I need a new black bag.' Sounds safe enough, doesn't it? In fact it sounds positively lovely. He can help you out with your shopping choices. You'll guide him towards that shirt you keep seeing in the windows at Selfridges that he would look drop-dead sexy in. Then you'll stop for a coffee and perhaps a delicate French pastry. You'll stroll in the sunshine, hand in hand, and exchange smug smiles with other happy, stylish couples who've also popped into town to update their wardrobes. You get to indulge in your two biggest passions. Him and Oxford Street.

Apart from, it's not quite like that. It's a wet weekend in January and you've managed to pick the opening of the sales for the setting of your first shop together. The trains are packed and the queues are ridiculous. But you're still enjoying yourself. You've battled through the crowds to secure that bargain pair of sandals you've had your eye on for the past few months. Yes, you nearly committed assault-with-intent in the process, but now they are yours. Who cares if they're two sizes too small? Once you start your new diet they'll be fine . . . You've rooted through the rails of rubbish with perseverance, determination and downright blood thirst. And it's paid off. Soon, your credit card will be feeling the weight of three pairs of shoes, two pairs of jeans, six evening tops and a lovely beaded cardigan that you just had to have. You're bruised, battered, exhausted, but it was all worth it. And the boyfriend? You've not entirely sure how his day's been really. He deserted you in the first shop when 'that #*@!*ing shop assistant took twenty-three minutes to get you a size twelve!'

Now surely if you two have made a decision to be a couple, you must have some things in common. You must have some common ground. So why are your interests so different? And why does he find it so hard to appreciate the things you love? If he loves you, then why he can't love your shoe collection too?

Well, if the question is 'Does he understand my passion for shopping?', then the answer is a big, fat resounding No. And it's not because he's selfish, single-minded or uninterested. In general, men just feel differently about shopping. To start with, there's the hard statistics. Research has concluded that upon trying on a pair of jeans, 65 per cent of men will buy them. And the women? Only 25 per cent will buy the first pair they try on. And that leaves a lot of scope for trying on jeans all day every day for weeks on end. A shopping researcher, Underhill, says, 'Shopping is still, and always will be, mostly for females. Shopping *is* female.' He says this is primarily due to evolution and the traditional 'hunter-gatherer' set up. So, prehistoric women were far more concerned with the finer details of berries, nuts and roots, while the men had the more general task of tracking down the nearest woolly mammoth, spearing it and dragging it home for supper. Then, as shopping evolved and we began to see grocery stores develop, shopping was what got women out of the house. It became an expedition away from the home and, occasionally, away from the children. Women became expert shoppers, expert choosers and expert decision makers. They became experts of brands, logos, types and varieties.

Admittedly, this relationship between women and shopping has taken another turn. With equality comes the fact that, for most women, their social contact and place in commerce and industry, stretches far beyond picking up a loaf of bread and a can of beans in the local grocer's. Shopping is no longer an escape from the home, because so many of us spend so little time actually in our homes anyway. It has become something we have to squeeze in rather than something to pad out our daily routine. But it is still a pastime that women enjoy far more than men. As Underhill concludes, 'For many women there are psychological and emotional aspects to shopping that are just plain absent in most men.'

In conclusion, the fact is that, no, he doesn't share your passion for shoe-shopping. And if he doesn't now, then he probably never will. Because, generally, men just don't. For a million and one different reasons, some of which we've discussed, to him, a black t-shirt is a black t-shirt. A blue skirt is a blue skirt. Hemlines, accessories, stitching, embroidery and fabrics are details lost on most men. So whereas you feel like you've had a productive day and have tried on the full range of new-season fashions, he feels like he's just seen you try on 367 denim skirts. And that was before he deserted you to go home to watch the football . . .

Here's what to do about it

So what does this mean? Are you and Mr Right destined to spend every weekend apart indulging your individual passions? Will you be one of those couples that are married on paper, but live in separate homes and socialise in different circles? Perhaps you should just call the whole thing off. If you can't even spend a little leisure time with your man, then what's the point of the whole palaver in the first place? And the answer is you can see it like this, or you can learn to accept that just because he doesn't have a passion for L.K. Bennett, it doesn't mean that he doesn't have a passion for you.

Part of coming to a relationship as a whole, rather than expecting someone else to complete you, means that you will have different interest and hobbies. And whether he's a football fanatic, a train spotter or a stamp collector, that's part of who he is. His passions are as much a part of him as his great eyes, his fab abs and his kind nature. So don't deny him them. Equally, this means you are free to indulge in your greatest loves. Now, just because you both want to do different things, it doesn't mean you have to do them together. If his idea of hell on earth is a shopping centre on a Saturday afternoon, then why force him to endure it? If you really want his input, then ask him to accompany you for a couple of hours after football. That way, you can do the groundwork research and break it down to a choice between two tops and a skirt, while he sweats it out on the pitch before meeting you to help with the final decision. Likewise, if you feel that you want to share in his interests, then work out ways of doing it that you both enjoy. So while standing on a wet, windy terrace with a bunch of shouting, heckling football fans might not be your idea of fun, a night in watching the game on TV with nachos and a bottle of wine might fit the bill perfectly. Don't expect any full attention until the final whistle is blown, but it's only ninety minutes and then you've got him to yourself – well, if you can tear him away from the post-match analysis.

If you encourage his interests and strive to become involved with them, it's far more likely that he will attempt a greater understanding of the things that really turn you on. He probably still won't want to play Bag Carrier every Saturday, but he might be more willing to accompany you every now and then. That might mean that when he's bored you find him a good pub and pick him up later, but at least you'll be free to shop minus the soundtrack of tuts, sighs and whinges. Accept that within a relationship you will both have separate interests, and the implications of this, at worst, are that you might have to spend a little time apart. It doesn't mean that he doesn't respect you, or that he isn't interested. It means he's a normal human being with likes and dislikes.

QUICK TIPS

1. Don't fall for the myth that says that happy couples do *everything* together.
2. Respect his alone time, and he'll be far more likely to respect yours.
3. Remember, you are dating a man not another woman.

He does, by genetic definition, see shopping (and everything else for that matter) differently to you.

Q. How come he finds it so difficult to be romantic?

Here's what's happening and why

It's a classic problem. At the beginning you can't get through your front door for all the flowers, cards and 'Just because' presents. Your email provider is screaming at you to get an upgrade because it can't cope with the sixty-five love e-letters a day (and that's not even including the thirty-five daily bunches of virtual flowers). You've chosen a favourite song, a favourite film, a favourite place and even a favourite colour, because you agree on *everything* now. There's surprise dinners, surprise dates and surprise days out. In fact you've begun to lose sight of the ironic twist to the saying 'Who says romance is dead?' Because it's not to you. Oh no. That ole devil called love has well and truly got you, and he popped into a florist on the way.

It's a lovely moment when you realise that your man knows what you want before you do, because before you realise what you want, it's been delivered, gift wrapped and sealed with a kiss. Surprise. Thought. Effort. All key characteristics of the type of gestures we have come to associate with those first few flushes of a new romance. You love the spontaneity of that impulse riverboat ride along the Thames. You love the way he's carved your initials into that tree at the bottom of his garden. And you love, love, love that he knows exactly how long you've been together. To the hour. And probably to the minute. So what's the problem? Well, the problem comes when you begin harassing the postman because he hasn't delivered your normal quota of love letters. The problem begins when you find yourself dropping hints as subtle as bus crashes so he will just buy you something, anything. The problem with a bit of lovey-dovey cuddly romance is when it stops.

So suddenly you wake up to find that your man isn't lovingly gazing at you like he used to. But his smelly boxers are strewn on the pillow next to you, so you deduce that he's had his morning shower because you certainly didn't rip them off in a fit of passion. You look down and realise that your breakfast actually hasn't been laid out beautifully on a tray at the foot of your bed and decorated with rose petals. So, a little despondent, you march downstairs to find that a culinary feast has indeed been prepared. There are pots and pans everywhere. The smell of smoky bacon and poached eggs fills the air. You rejoice! He has cooked a delicious breakfast! 'Good morning, darling, where's mine?' you politely enquire. He manages to drag his eyes from the GMTV sofa for long enough to inform you that, unfortunately, there wasn't anything left, because he was *really hungry*, but he thinks there is some cereal left in the cupboard if you want to go out and buy some milk. Superb. You try another tack. Perhaps you could meet up for a picnic lunch in the park today? No, he's too busy. Perhaps he'd like to go out for dinner tonight? No, he's meeting the boys at the pub. Maybe at the weekend he'd like to go away for a bit and stay in a nice hotel somewhere? No, too expensive, 'But we can borrow Mum and Dad's caravan if you're going to nag about getting away.' Charming.

There are no cards. The presents have stopped. And the last flowers you received from him have long been relocated to the bin. He doesn't surprise you. You don't surprise him. And big romantic gestures have become things that 'other couples do'. So where has the romance gone? Suddenly he's gone from being the world's greatest romantic to being one of those grunting, uncaring slobs that you always thought existed only in the form of your friends' boyfriends. If there was a soundtrack to your relationship, somebody has taken out the Stevie Wonder CD and stuck on a bit of Eminem.

Here's what to do about it

Has your boyfriend left his crystal ball lying around lately? Perhaps you've seen some tarot cards at the bottom of his gym bag? No? Then why do you assume he's psychic? One of the biggest mistakes we make when trying to read a man's behaviour is assuming that he can read our minds. You don't want to have to *tell* him that you need him to be more romantic. He should just *know*. Well, look at it from his point of view. He met this great girl. He wanted to prove that he was worthy of being with her. So he pulled out all the stops. There were flowers. There were recipe books so he could fool you into believing that 'La cheese sur la toast' wasn't his only culinary capability. He even bought a new shirt just because you casually remarked that red was your favourite colour and his wardrobe previously consisted of a spectrum from blue to grey and back to blue again. He was smitten and he wanted you to know it. Then, to his great surprise, he actually managed to snag this amazing, amazing girl. Result! And suddenly he didn't feel like he had to impress you 24/7. He began feeling comfortable, and relaxed, and content. He's secure enough to know that you don't need chocolates, bouquets and Barry Manilow CDs. And he's loving every minute.

Meanwhile, we completely misinterpret this stage as the end of the honeymoon period, the beginning of the end, and a sign that he's losing interest at a rate of knots. The only way to clear this up is to talk to him. Make it clear that you feel the way you do. Let him know that you still want to feel special and spoiled occasionally. Don't set up romantic expectations in your mind and then blame him when he fails to meet them. Tell him that it would be nice if, every now and then, he made the kind of gestures that he made at the beginning. You don't want him to spend a fortune on some grand overblown romantic gesture that he thinks you want. You just want him to do something that shows a little thought (although if forced to mount a beautiful white horse and ride to an empty castle just before a sexy thunderstorm breaks out, you would comply). The point is that you can't expect him to know that you still want a little romance if you don't tell him.

Whatever you do, don't keep your frustration to yourself, because all you'll do is convince yourself that he's not interested, he's not attracted to you and, in the words of The Righteous Brothers, he really has lost that loving feelin'. Don't internalise his lack of romance, because it will only make you feel bad about yourself and your own self-worth when in reality, the situation probably has nothing to do with that. Losing a little of that initial spark is normal in any relationship, but make sure you let him know that just occasionally you would like to feel like a new couple again. This might mean going on 'dates'. It might mean breakfast in bed every now and then. It might just mean leaving the newspaper open on the page he knows you like best. The clearer you are about your expectations, the more likely it is that they will be met.

QUICK TIPS

1. Why does *he* always have to make all the effort? Try surprising him with his favourite meal or a big night out. He'll feel special and it'll give him some hints too . . .
2. When he does make a romantic gesture, get excited. Do not say, 'Well, it's about bloody time . . .'
3. After two months, those flowers are most probably dead. Throw them away. They smell. Perhaps then he'll realise it's time for the next surprise . . .

Q. Why is it taking forever for him to introduce me to his parents?

Here's what's happening and why

You know his parents are important to him. Admittedly, at first you found the picture of them that's hung above his bed a *little* bit creepy. But, with time, you've come to realise that it's just a sign of his love and respect for his mum and dad. He quotes his dad when he's explaining important issues, and he still likes things cooked 'just the way my mum used to do it'. And you've always found it fairly endearing. So what if he's a bit of a mummy's boy? His respect for her shows a general respect for women and an acknowledgement of the importance of family. Which is all fairly attractive stuff, after all.

And you know you're important to him. He tells you as much. You're spending a lot of time together, you've moved past the stage of casual dating and you even hold hands in public now – all the time. Brilliant. Apart from, there's one little niggling issue. If his parents are so important to him, and you're important to him, why has he got such a problem with you all meeting? It's become ridiculous. You feel like some weird stalker trying desperately to weasel your way into his family home against his wishes. At every given opportunity you offer to give him a lift to pick something up from home, or meet him at his family gathering before you go out for dinner – you know, if it's easier. You're not even that bothered about meeting his parents, but the fact that he is so against it has lit and consequently fuelled a thirst that you're fairly sure is uncommon in a right-minded individual. You can't understand his reluctance. What's the big deal?

The reason it's a big deal to you is the very same reason that it's a big deal to him. The phrase 'meeting the parents' has acquired far more than its actual meaning. It has become symbolic of something much more serious. Introducing your parents to a partner doesn't just say, 'Oh, by the way, this is my dad, Bob,' it says, 'I'm at a stage where I consider our relationship important enough to inform my family about. I am proud that you are my partner, and I want you to meet my parents because they, too, are very special to me. Oh, and by the way, this is my dad, Bob – would you like a fondant fancy?' And because of all the reasons we've talked about – fear of commitment, fear of change and a little bit of relationship claustrophobia – steps like this can be really, really scary. Just like moving in together, sending joint Christmas cards and getting engaged, 'meeting the parents' can feel like a massive relationship advance. As we've discussed, men are often less likely to want to make these big commitments than women, because of their evolutionary and sociological background. And, at a most basic level, think of the reaction that he'll get from his mates down the pub when he decides to reveal that he's going to let you 'meet the family'. 'Well, mate, that's it now, marriage is next' or 'Oh, that'll be the end of your Sundays down the pub now! She'll get you under lock and key – it'll be family dinners and quiet nights in with the folks from now on!' It's no wonder he's running scared . . .

So, if you feel like you want to meet his parents because it will drive your relationship to the next level, you need to appreciate that he might also feel that it will change your relationship, and that's exactly why he'd rather you and his folks remained strangers. And this isn't necessarily a huge deal. In the first few weeks and months, is it really a big problem whether you get to meet his parents or not? After all, this time is when you need to get to know each other really well. Not each other's parents. It's not highly inappropriate if you haven't met his parents after two months. But if seven or eight months on you still haven't had an afternoon with Mummy and Daddy, gazing at embarrassing baby photos, perhaps it's time to take matters into your own hands. Don't wait until he's at work and then raid his address book, track down his family home and force your way in. There are a couple of more rational (and more legal) ways to do it . . .

Here's what to do about it

Before you launch into a long lecture about commitment to the relationship, his pride in you and the feeling that he'd rather that you and his folks were not so much in different rooms but on different continents, you need to look at your own behaviour. Have you actually given him any indication that you want to meet his parents? Does he know it's important to you? And finally, is there any way you can back this up by showing him how you would like things to be moving, rater than just telling him? Because one of the best ways to encourage him to make a move like this is to make the move yourself. It's what psychologists call 'modelling behaviour'. It's what everyone else calls 'leading by example'. So set up a situation where he can get to know *your* family. And don't make it a big deal. If you run home and say, 'Oh my God! We need to go shopping! And we need to get your hair cut! And stand up straight! You're meeting my family tomorrow, and if they didn't like you it would be awful. My dad nearly ate my last boyfriend alive!' then you might find your other half a little anxious. If you say, 'Oh, my mum and dad are having a little do for their anniversary on Saturday and I thought we could pop in before we go out for dinner?' then he might not even notice you slyly arranging his first appointment with your family. And once he sees that it's not that scary, he'll be far more likely to reciprocate. By asking him to meet your parents, you are showing him how you think the relationship should be moving and what you feel comfortable with. It's a great way of showing him what you expect, or would like, without having to actually say anything at all.

This, however, is assuming that he does agree to meet your parents. What if it's not just you meeting his family that he has a problem with? What if your 'behaviour modelling' doesn't really pay off because he doesn't like your behaviour in the first place and he won't comply with it? Your plans to ease his fears by showing him how laid back 'meeting the parents' can be might just fall apart if he's sitting at home, refusing to leave the house. Well, in this situation you really do need to confront the issue with him. Be clear and direct. Say, 'I'd really love to meet your parents. Is there a reason I haven't?' And remember that confronting issues head-on like this means that you also take the risk of receiving a clear, direct answer. And it might not be the answer you were hoping for. Prepare yourself for an answer like 'I don't feel ready', and acknowledge that the next step might need to be a little soul searching about where your relationship is actually heading.

Be honest with yourself about the similarities and, more importantly, the differences in the way you and him are viewing the relationship. If it constantly feels like an uphill struggle to convince him to make little gestures of commitment, then are you sure he actually wants to commit to you? When dealing with a relationship-progress issue like this, be rational, be reasonable, but be honest. If you're ready to take the next step and he's not, even after a discussion and a clear example from you, then maybe he's not the man you need to be taking these steps with anyway.

QUICK TIPS

1. Set a good example and ask if he wants to meet your family first.

2. Be calm. If he's worried about commitment, screaming at him like a mad banshee about going to golf with your dad will not help settle his nerves.
3. Don't try to engineer 'chance' meetings in the supermarket. He'll see through it and question your sanity. As should you.

Q. He was really into sex in the beginning, but he isn't any more. Does he still find me sexy?

Here's what's happening and why

At first you could do no wrong. If you burped it was cute. If you fell over, it was endearing. If you got horrendously drunk and vomited in the toilets for three hours, it was still sexy. Strangely enough. You used to greet him in your ex-boyfriend's boxer shorts, a manky old vest and a hair-do that has not been seen in public since Tina Turner realised that even *Private Dancers* can afford to go to a hair stylist who is at least partially sighted. Your breath smelt, your skin looked awful and your legs were hairier than his, yet still he scooped you up in his arms and whisked you off to bed. Once he had removed a face-full of the bouffant monstrosity on your head . . . Hell, you couldn't even get up for your morning shower without the combination of you in a towel and him in boxers meaning that you ended up straight back in bed again. Sex wasn't something you had to scramble to find time for – it was something you based the rest of your daily routine around.

So how on earth did you get to where you are now? Sitting in bed with the same man, not passionately kissing, not ripping each other's clothes off, not whispering sweet nothings. You're reading your star signs for next week, and he's completing a crossword. You've got your massive bed socks on as very sexy accessories to your fleecy pyjamas, because it's getting 'a bit nippy at night'. He's wearing the same stinky t-shirt he's been wearing all day, with the same over-washed, faded boxers he's been sporting since he was fifteen and they were his 'pulling pants'. You decide to try a little kiss on the cheek. No reaction. You hold his hand. He humours you for a few seconds, and then drags his hand away so he can fill in '18 across'. Wow. It's like *Basic Instinct*, *Eyes Wide Shut* and *Fatal Attraction* all rolled into one. It's amazing that you can actually contain your excitement . . .

So why does it have to change? Why do we have to go from nearly-X-rated love scenes to crosswords in bed? Why can't it all be like it was at the beginning, forever and ever? Because it can't. Because when things are new to us, of course they are more exciting, more lust-filled, more frantic, but they are like that *because* they are new. So, by definition, things absolutely can't remain the way they were in the beginning when you were ripping clothes, waking neighbours and breaking beds. Because eventually things stop being new. And anyway, it would be physically and mentally impossible to be *permanently* excited, and sustain a sex life that would make Hugh Hefner jealous, forever. And that doesn't mean that you might as well go out and start looking at sets of single beds, and burn your sexy undies now. The change of pace and energy in your relationship can be a good thing. Because, more often than not, it means your relationship is turning into something more solid and just as special. Most relationships go through this period of crystallisation. While your feelings for each other might not have changed, they may have solidified into something that is less intense. Think about it being like a beautiful piece of jewellery – like the ring your mum bought you for your twenty-first. At first, you absolutely, madly, deeply love it. You want to wear it everywhere and anywhere. You feel excited whenever somebody asks you the time, and you start taking three hours to sign credit slips, pay for tube tickets and shake hands, because you want *everybody* to notice. Every time you take the ring off you can't wait to put it back on again. But eventually that kind of lust begins to fade. You still love your ring, but it has been relegated a little further into your jewellery box. And, if you're honest, it just doesn't give you the same frenzied excitement. So what do you do? Do you give up on it? Do you throw it away? Of course not. You think of different ways to update it. You follow Carrie Bradshaw's lead and wear it round your neck. You have the stones made into earrings. You experiment with it and keep it interesting. And that's exactly what you have to do with your sex life.

Here's what to do about it

'Spicing up' your love life might sound like the kind of clichéd advice you associate with your mother's generation, but the fact is that you both need to put effort into keeping your relationship exciting all the way through, not just when you're old enough to draw your pension. And 'updating' your sex life doesn't mean that you have to change it beyond recognition. So don't think that a trip to your local sex shop is the answer. Whips, chains and hot wax might be your thing, but if it isn't you might just send him running for the hills as opposed to the bedroom. No, keeping your sex life interesting just means that you need to put a little more effort in.

So change locations, go away for the weekend. It's amazing what the difference can be between a bed in your messy bedroom and a bed in a classy hotel room. It's exciting because it's a sign that you're both acknowledging how important it is to make time for each other, and you're both putting in a little effort to keep your sex life interesting. Make little changes to your lifestyle that will make it that little bit more sexy – take baths together, leave notes for each other. Remember the things you used to do before the days when sex became something 'other people did'. Don't fall into the trap of sitting around together watching TV – try to keep 'dating' so that you still want to make yourself look good for each other. To keep things alive you need to keep putting this effort in, and avoid becoming complacent.

And if he's always the one that initiates sex, and the reason you two simply aren't doing it as much is because he hasn't made a move in ages, then why not be the one to start things up for a change? He'll appreciate the effort you're making and he'll probably love the fact that, for once, it's you initiating sex not him.

Make sure you don't internalise the issue and blame yourself. The trap many women fall into at this point in a relationship is thinking that they have acquired a brand new skill. They kid themselves that they've attended some kind of course, obtained an internationally-recognised qualification, and they prepare to make the necessary alterations to their CV. 'I have a full, clean driving licence, a keen interest in tap-dancing, oh – and the ability to mind read.' So we interpret and we analyse, and we pull out the old crystal ball and arrive at conclusions that don't necessarily bear any resemblance to reality, but do match up with the scenarios we have created in our heads. And then we match up his behaviour to further support our latest theory. So the reason sex has dwindled must be because he thinks we're unattractive. Then, if he can't pick us up from work, we imagine that it's because he'll be embarrassed to be seen with us in public, because he finds us so physically disgusting. Or, if he prepares a beautiful salad for dinner, we assume that it's his way of trying to con us into losing weight so that he might possibly fancy us again.

The fact is that there are a million reasons why your sex life might have diminished, and his disappearing attraction to you is just one explanation. Maybe you've reached the crystallisation process of your relationship where the intensity and madness of the first flush of romance begins to settle into something a little more controlled? Maybe he's just really stressed out with work and he's finding it hard to focus on other things like you, right now, because he's so distracted? Maybe he's holding back a bit because he's picking up on your new insecurities and he's not quite sure how to deal with them?

Speak to him. You need a little more reassurance from him. You need more frequent validation and, basically, more attention from him. That doesn't make you needy, greedy or a spoilt brat. It just means that you still want to feel special and sexy and attractive to a man who means a lot to you. Just expressing this to him is a major step in achieving it. If you've noticed that your sex life has dwindled, then he probably has too. So, ask him if he's happy with things in the bedroom. And then, between you, you should be able to come up with some ways to make your bedtime stories a little more Jackie Collins, and a little less Ordnance Survey.

QUICK TIPS

1. Keep the lines of communication open. If you think things have dwindled, then maybe he does too.
2. Be ready for a little drop in sexual activity. It's only natural after those first few weeks or months.
3. If all else fails: chain him up. Maybe that's what he's been waiting for. Or maybe not. It's a risk you take . . .

Q. Why does he need female friends when he has me?

Here's what's happening and why

You feel like you want to give your man everything he needs. Of course you do. It's why you try to whip up his favourite meals on a regular basis. It's why you spend Sunday mornings shivering on the sidelines of the local football pitch. It's why you spend Sunday evenings listening to a minute-by-minute analysis of exactly why that second-half corner didn't find its way to the back of the net. And he seems to be fairly happy. You look after him well. So why on earth does he need other women in his life? Yes, you accept his mother's involvement. After all, she put the groundwork into making him the man he is today (although you can't help but think that your life would be easier if she'd made him wash up a little more). Then there are his sisters, and they're fine too, because largely they stick up for you when he's having a tantrum. The women he works with are OK too, after all he has to talk to them and you're sure it's only about accounts and figures and gross profit and boring things like that anyway. But why does he need Sam, his first girlfriend from school? Or Jo, that girl he worked with about a million years ago? They don't give any of the things that his family or his colleagues do, they're just added extras. Surely you can give him all the female perspective that he needs in his life? You accept that he needs to spend time with the boys, and that they provide him with something you can't. Like drinking competitions, dirty jokes and shaving-foam related torture when he passes out on a Friday night. But these women? Why does he need them? Surely he must just fancy them? And clearly he's biding his time with you so he can eventually run off into the sunset with one of them? You're no fool: you've seen *When Harry Met Sally* . . .

Well, no, not quite. There's probably far more to it than that. Studies have found that men benefit more from friendships with women than the women do. This is because a group of women will talk about their thoughts and feelings, and a group of men tend to stick to subjects such as sport and work. So you won't find a group of men talking about their deepest, darkest fears and desires. Unless one of them happens to be Man United winning the premiership. So they often use their friendships with women as an outlet for some of the feelings that they just wouldn't discuss with their friends. So, as much as you picture them feeding each other ice cream in a Häagen Dazs-advert kind of way, he probably just uses his female friends to listen to some of his fears and concerns.

Which is all great, but you can't help thinking that he

should be able to do this with you. After all you're a woman. And not only that, you're a woman who he chooses to spend the majority of his time with. And how many times have you heard lovestruck partners gush, 'She's not just my lover, she's also my best friend'? You want to be his best friend, so you can't quite understand why he needs any other women around. So how do you get around this? How do you confront him with it? And what do you do if he doesn't react in exactly the way you want, which at the moment is getting rid of any friends that don't talk about cars, boobs and football?

Here's what to do about it

Firstly, you need to accept that the majority of your fears are probably entirely unfounded. The idea that men and women can't be friends is an outdated hang-over from history. There was an era when women and men didn't know if a platonic friendship could actually exist, because they never got a chance to find out. The women were in the home, while men were out earning the family's money. Men got to socialise with men and women got to socialise with women, and the only real excuse for hanging out together was if there were romantic intentions involved.

The word 'platonic' originates from the philosopher Plato, who first came up with the idea of a love, or deep connection, that was free from sexual attraction. Originally, the word was intended to describe the type of relationship individuals would have with God. However, in recent years the word has come to describe a non-sexual relationship between a man and a woman. And since the days of women at the sink and men at their desks have pretty much passed into oblivion, psychologists have come to accept that this type of relationship can and does exist. This is because with equality, men and women are more likely to be in a position to work together more frequently. Also, the development of equality has meant that the lines between male and female are becoming more blurred, as both assume roles that are less defined by gender. So men are more sensitive and emotional – after all, if it's ok for Gazza to cry his eyes out over a football game, then so can your man. And women have become more assertive. These similarities and merging of characteristics mean that men and women are more likely to find common ground and socialise in similar ways.

So the first thing you need to do is try and ignore your fears that platonic friendships are up there with flying pigs, Father Christmas and men who call when they say they will. Your boyfriend socialises with women because he enjoys their company, not because he wants to get into their knickers. Be logical, if he really wanted to be with Jo from the office or Sally from the gym, and not you, then wouldn't he just do it? And the fact that you're a female does not mean that you can fulfil every one of his friendship needs. Think about your own friends, you love them all for different reasons. You love being with Ros because she's such a good laugh. You love Kerry because she's such a caring listener. And that's exactly how he probably feels about his own friends. You're his girlfriend and he thinks you're great for a million different reasons, but he can't talk about primary school with you like he can with his childhood friend Sophie. He can't laugh about the same smutty jokes with you as he can with Bonnie from the pub. And he can't be the relationship agony uncle with you in the same way he can with his eternally-single friend Lucy. You need to accept that – wait for it, take a seat – these women might provide him with something you can't. That doesn't mean that you've failed, or that you should be intimidated. It means that you carry on being the woman he's chosen to share the majority of his life with, and you give him the freedom to enjoy time with people who just fulfil those little needs that aren't really your speciality.

Another big fear is that he might, shock horror, be talking to his female friends about you. And that, even worse, it might not all be exactly positive. It can be quite unsettling when you have the mother of all rows and then you overhear him talking to one of his female friends about it. The answer to this is not to try and kid yourself that he doesn't voice his concerns about your relationship to his friends, but to come to terms with the fact that he probably does talk to them like this and it's not the end of the world. In fact it's a good thing. The fact that he talks to others about you is a sign that you are an important part of his life.

We've mentioned the fact that researchers have concluded that men actually get a lot from friendships with women because they are more likely to talk to them about fears and worries. So, if he's worried about things between you two, then he may well talk to his girlfriends about it. And although you may have visions of them pouting with disgust at his tales of your horrendous behaviour, the reality is probably very different. Think about it. These people are women. They are more likely to think in a similar way to you. And when he moans about how unfair it is that you don't want him to spend every single night polishing his car in the garage, or down the pub, or on his computer, his friends are more likely than he is to see your point of view.

The truth is, females can be great proponents for the girl in a guy's life. They can give him a girl's perspective and help him to see your side of the argument. Make the most of them. It's even better if you can build some kind of relationship with them yourself. Yes, let them be his friends, but if they can meet you every now and then, they'll be more likely to fight your corner when he's having a little moan.

The key here is just to recognise that he needs people other than you in his life. Imagine if all of your male friends suddenly ditched you because their new girlfriend didn't like them having female friends. You would think it was ridiculous. Likewise, imagine if your man told you to dump all of your male friends. You would probably be horrified, because without your friends around you would feel as if something was missing from your life. Acknowledge that this is how he feels too, and learn to accept that although you can provide him with so many things, you can't give him everything.

QUICK TIPS

1. Don't slag off his female friends in the vain attempt that it might force him to reconsider his relationship with them. It won't. It might make him reconsider his relationship with you.
2. If you have male friends, then remember how important they are to you, and imagine how you'd feel if he tried to stop you seeing them.

3. Make friends with his friends – get them on side. Then, if he does talk about your relationship to them, they're far more likely to stick up for you.

Q We keep having the same arguments. How do we stop going round in circles?

Here's what's happening and why

The phrase 'broken record' has never sounded so apt. In fact your life would be far easier if you could just record the phrases, 'Please do the washing up, – because other-wise I'll have to do it' and 'I'm going to my mum's!' and play them on repeat – perhaps with the addition of some sound effects, including a couple of slammed doors and a few smashed plates. Because that's all your evenings seem to consist of at the moment. If there's housework to be done, you can bet there's an argument to be had about it.

You can remember a time when you would wander into a spotless flat, and if the little angel had left a plate or two festering in the living room you were more than happy to clean up after him. But now? Now a discarded take-away dish is justification enough for an argument on the same scale as a world war. As you walk through the door, you spy the dish – you catch his eye, he catches yours. And in that split second, you both know. You both just know that tonight is going to be one of those nights. It doesn't matter how long you put it off for. Sure, try and ignore the offending chicken-chow-mein carton, distract yourself with terse questions about how his day was, but you both know that sooner or later it's all going to kick off. And some stage in the next hour, the latest in your series of epic disagreements will take place.

Or perhaps it occurs when you're out and about. You're out with friends, having a good night. He's buying the drinks, which is always good, so you're relaxed and having fun. Then you see it. Your blood boils, and you're fairly sure that steam is coming out of your nose. Yet again, just when he thought you were too preoccupied with your girlie cocktail, you catch him staring at a stunning girl in a very, very revealing boob tube and mini skirt combo. She doesn't notice, but you sure as hell do. Suddenly, your wonderful, caring boyfriend has turned into the sleaze at the bar. OK, so he's stopped looking now, and he's far more focused on paying for the drinks and getting them back to the table, but that's not the point. You won't say anything now. Oh no, right now he's getting the tense silences and moody-glare treatment. Just as a warning shot, so he knows it's coming too. And then later on, the gloves are off: it's round two.

It can be really easy to get dragged into a circle where you feel like you are just having the same old arguments over and over again. After your three-hundred-and-seventy-fifth argument about dirty dishes or his wandering eye or your constant lateness, it can feel like you are destined to spend your life screaming at each other. But the key to escaping is to break the cycle that, between you, you have established. And this might sound like one of those easier-said-than-done things, but it can be done. For the sake of your crockery . . .

Here's what to do about it

The first step to resolving any argument is to establish exactly what it is that you're arguing about. This sounds simple, but the immediate answer is probably 'the dishes', or 'him being controlling', or 'his smelly football boots'. Which, yes, on the surface, may well be the main topic of the disagreement, but really you need to look a little deeper than that. If a mouldy Chinese-takeaway box never bothered you in the beginning, why does it evoke a mad rage now? Because it has come to symbolise something else. That little foil box is no longer just a little foil box housing a couple of noodles and some black bean sauce. Oh no. It has come to mean a lack of respect, a blatant disregard for your feelings, an indicator of his declining love for you and a deliberate attempt to anger you. And that's what the argument is really about. The poor, defenceless takeaway box has got virtually nothing to do with it.

The reason that you keep going round in circles is because in trying to solve the arguments, you're just examining them at their most basic level. So you see the dishes, but you don't look at what it is that they mean to you or how they make you feel. So while you might be screaming, 'Clean up this filthy mess, you repulsive disgusting slob!' and a number of carefully chosen swear words, the one thing you're not saying is: 'I feel like you are completely disrespecting me when you leave my flat in such a mess. It hurts my feelings and makes me feel a little insecure, because it makes me think you don't care,' or 'I hate the way that when you don't clean up after yourself it makes me feel as if I am acting like your mother, and I don't like being put in that position. We should be equals in this relationship and I shouldn't have to dictate to you.'

You might be focusing on the problem at its most obvious level because, deep down, you fear addressing what the real issue is. Are you worried that if you confront him about how much he cares for you, the answer might not be what you want to hear?

It's far easier to scream and shout about pots and pans than it is to discuss heartfelt insecurities. But sometimes just being able to put these feelings into words, so that you are focusing on the actual problem and not all the other rubbish is all it takes to stop the cycle. Because upon hearing, 'Darling, why haven't you done the washing up?' he'll probably just start to filter you out – perhaps even turn the television up, so you're competing with Des Lynam (and we all know who's going to win that contest . . .). And he'll do that because he'll think you're about to burst into the same old argument about the same old thing. So break the cycle, and try having a discussion about what the real issue is.

QUICK TIPS

1. Stop beating around the bush. What are you really angry about?
2. Identify typical 'trigger' issues, and each time one comes up try to walk away and calm down before you confront him.
3. If your arguments are about really serious issues that violate your boundaries, consider whether this really is the right relationship for you.

Q. Why does he put me down in front of his friends?

Here's what's happening and why

Now, as we've said, the initial mad flurry of the first flushes of romance eventually subside to make way for something that is tougher, stronger and more solid, if a little less exciting. Your feelings crystallise and become more familiar, more secure and a little less intense. It means that when he walks through the door, laden with shopping bags, your initial thought changes from 'Oh my God! The way he is holding that Waitrose bag is so, soooo sexy and I haven't seen him for a whole three hours! Oh my God! I just need to have him *now*!' to something more like 'Oh bless him, he's done some shopping so I don't have to worry about dinner tonight.' It means that your standard sleepwear mysteriously transforms from a ribbed, boned negligee and Gina heels to fleece pyjamas and ski socks. And it means that his typical greeting may just change from 'Hi gorgeous, how are you? It's great to see you, you look amazing' to 'It's about time, I've been waiting here for donkey's years.'

As we become more comfortable in a relationship, we feel that we can relax a little because we feel more secure that the other person isn't going to do a runner at the slightest hint of any imperfections you may possess. We feel that we can get away with more because we're fairly sure the other person is in for the long haul. For you, this might mean letting your bikini line get a little unruly. For him, this might mean subjecting you to what he imagines is his legendary sense of humour. So, this sense of familiarity leads him to think that you will find his wise-cracks, in front of a bunch of his mates, about your slightly uncontrolled spending habits just as hysterical as they seem to. Which is fine, if you do. But if you don't, you could have a problem on your hands.

Because jokes about your weight or your job or your hair or your aforementioned spending habits might be merely mildly tedious when they're made in the comfort of your home, between you and him. But it can be an entirely different matter when you're surrounded by a bunch of clapping seals, otherwise known as his mates, in the pub. 'No love,' he jests, 'you're not fat, just a bit more cuddly!' Cue rapturous merriment. 'Now, I'm not saying my girlfriend's stupid, but the longest book she's ever read is *Vogue*!' Cue frenzied applause. 'She told me she loved me last night, so I told her to get on her back and prove it!' Cue hysterical chortling, wild jeering, lights down, curtain up and one hacked off girlfriend.

Now, if you're honest, your man's cheeky sense of humour is probably one of the things that attracted you to him in the first place. His 'fat' jokes were funny when they were aimed at his mate, Bob, or some stranger in the street. His 'blonde' jokes were great when they were aimed at his sister. And his 'stupid' jokes were your absolute favourites until they were fired at full throttle in your direction. While not wanting to appear the nagging girlfriend, you can't help feeling uncomfortable when the joke is on you and you're in front of a bloodthirsty audience. So why does he seem to enjoy putting you down in front of his mates so much? What happened to the days when he used to make you feel good about yourself? And is throwing a pint over him a suitable plan of action?

Here's what to do about it

There's good news and bad news here. The bad news is that people only put you down if they feel like they can. Therefore, somebody can only make you feel bad about yourself if you let them. So, if your boyfriend has got into the habit of launching a daily attack on your clothes, weight, job etc., etc., that is probably because you've let him get away with it for far too long already, so he's never really appreciated that it actually upsets you. Somewhere along the line you've given him the impression that it's OK to put you down. So while he might not be doing it with the express purpose of making you feel bad about yourself, he might just be doing it because he thinks you find it funny or that you actually enjoy it. As we've said before, men are far less adept at reading emotion and gauging responses than women. So the icy stare he receives after his latest crack about your mother may well be interpreted as a jovial pretence of annoyance or, more likely, he might not even notice it at all.

But the good news is that this also means that you are the one with the power to stop it, simply by making it clear that you don't find his comparisons between you and a beached whale particularly funny. And the best way to do this is just to be straightforward about it. Don't beat around the bush, don't mince your words, or do any other clichés that basically mean skirting around the real problem. If he's man enough to make jokes about you in front of his mates, then he's man enough to deal with an adult discussion about it. Again, he probably hasn't realised how uncomfortable it makes you feel, so a simple 'Stop it!' should do the trick. Explain that you want to enjoy spending time with him, not feel like you are lying in wait for the next shot of his hilarious insight into your ridiculous world. Speak to him about why this is happening. Perhaps his mates rib him about how serious your relationship is, and his little put-downs are his way of convincing them that he has the upper hand and he's not that serious about you after all. Pathetic but possible. Maybe he feels like you're not as into him as you used to be, and he's just attention seeking. Whatever the reason, the first step is undoubtedly to make sure that he knows that this is actually upsetting you, then you can get down to the reasons why and set about stopping it.

If asking him to stop isn't enough, and you still feel like your self-esteem has done ten rounds with Mike Tyson, then perhaps you need to look at why. Relationships are not necessities, they are added bonuses, and the best reason to be in one is because it makes us feel good about ourselves. If there's an aspect of your life you're not entirely happy with – for example, your appearance, your weight or your career – your man should be able to put these worries into perspective and make you feel better about them, not highlight them. If you've asked your boyfriend to stop putting you down in front of people and he continues, knowing how it upsets you, you need to ask yourself why you are putting up with it. You deserve far more from a relationship, and if this man is not delivering on that then perhaps it's time to say goodbye.

QUICK TIPS

1. Learn the difference between you being too sensitive because you've had a bad day, and him really pushing it too far. Or he'll just get confused.

2. Next time he makes another hysterical joke, level one back at him. Good targets include his football abilities . . .

3. If, after a frank discussion, he persists, look seriously at how happy the relationship is making you.

Q. I think he still has feelings for his ex, what should I do?

Here's what's happening and why

Of course you're pleased that he and his ex had such an amicable break-up. You're delighted that they can still go out for dinner. You're relieved that she's such a nice person, because it reinforces your belief in his excellent choice in women. You love that he is so comfortable with her new boyfriend, clearly demonstrating a lack of jealousy, bitterness and any other nasty ex-relationship feelings. And you're proud that making time for her is so important to him, because it just shows how loyal and dependable he is. But you still wish she would vanish off the face of the earth.

You know it's childish, you know it's insecure, you know it's a little bit unnecessary, but you can't help but worry that there is something else going on. He speaks so highly of her and you can see why. Annoyingly, she's beautiful, successful, sexy and amazingly nice. In fact, if you weren't in a relationship, you'd date her yourself. Well, maybe. And clearly there is still a special little bond between them. How could there not be? No matter how hard they try to include you in their conversations, how could you possibly share in their enthusiastic memories of that night in Rome when they danced in the street to a lone violinist? How can you possibly cackle with the same hysteria as they recall the day they had a paint fight while redecorating her flat? How can you speculate on the marriage difficulties of their friends Rob and Sarah, when you've never actually met Rob and Sarah? The saying 'two's company, three's a crowd' never felt more apt . . .

It's not that you don't trust your man, and it's not that you think he would ever cheat on you. But then that's not what you're really scared of. You're not worried that on one of their lunches they're going to suddenly surrender to an overwhelming lust and start rolling around in the Harvester beer garden. You know she's devoted to her man, and you know that your man is devoted to you. What you're scared of, what really keeps you up at night, is the horrible, niggling feeling that he still loves her. The fear that he might *want* to reignite the flame with her is far greater than the fear that he would actually *do* it. After all, he can stop himself from falling into bed with her, but if he still has feelings for her then there's not a lot he, or you for that matter, can do about it.

So how do you know whether your fears are rational or ridiculous? Are you acting like a green-eyed bunny boiler or are your concerns justified? And what if broaching the subject with him confirms your worst fears? Well, you have two choices here. You can confront him and get to the bottom of the issue, good or bad, establishing his true feelings and therefore giving your relationship a far more honest and secure framework to work from. Or, you can shirk the issue and completely avoid the topic, just in case he says, 'Yes, I still have feelings for her.' Oh, and you'll drive yourself into a mad, deep state of paranoia, where every lunch is a secret meeting to discuss your demise and every hug is a lust-filled signal of desire and immense longing. Time to confront him then . . .

Here's what to do about it

It's hard to get this one right. While you want to seem nonchalant, reasonable and in control, it is, of course, far too easy to sound paranoid, obsessive and downright scary. But the first thing to do is to assure yourself that these feelings of jealousy are perfectly understandable. A certain amount of jealousy is completely natural and doesn't necessarily mean you've lost the plot. So bear this in mind when you approach the topic with him. Don't think that asking him about his ex will make you seem like a mad stalker: it won't, providing you do it in the right way.

That means no shouting, screaming or swearing. It means thinking about questions that will encourage him to see things from your point of view, rather than making him feel like he is being accused. So, 'Do you fancy Tina?' will not work as well as 'You and Tina have been seeing a lot of each other lately, is there any reason for that?' or 'I don't know how you and Tina managed to stay such great friends, break-ups can be really hard. How do you do it?' If you're feeling brave then tell him that, occasionally, you feel a little uncomfortable with how close he and his ex-girlfriend are, tell him that you probably just need a little reassurance that their relationship has no bearing on yours.

And the answer to your questions probably won't be in what he says, it'll be in the way he reacts. If your fears are completely unfounded, he will probably be completely oblivious to why you are asking. Because the thought of him running of with his ex-girlfriend has probably never occurred to him. You'll know in the instant that he begins to answer the question exactly how justified your fears are. And if he is calm, caring and helps extinguish any insecurities you may have, then you need to accept that there probably isn't anything going on. Put things in perspective. If your boyfriend had these deep, unresolved feelings for his ex-girlfriend, then why on earth would he be wasting his time with you. Remember that no matter how thick the lenses are in the rose-tinted glasses that they're looking at their relationship through now, it couldn't have been all that perfect. They broke up. And he chose to be with you. Look at their friendship as a good thing. Isn't it better that he can have an adult, amicable relationship with his ex-girlfriend, rather than snarling and hissing at the mere mention of her name? Now that would be a sign of unresolved feelings . . .

If, however, his reaction isn't quite what you were hoping for, then you might find yourself feeling even worse about the situation. If he is *too* defensive, *too* adamant or just plain angry, then this could well be a sign that he does have unresolved issues with his ex-girlfriend. Now, you really need to be clear here. And that means being clear about exactly what you want to hear and what needs to happen for you to feel happier with the situation. If you approach him with 'The way you just reacted tells me that something is going on', then his instant, automatic reactions will probably be 'No, there isn't', and you'll hit a brick wall straightaway. Rather than accusing him, lay out some foundations for what you expect him to do in order to ease your fears. And here are a few pointers. Insisting that he allows you to listen to every single one of their phone calls is not an effective strategy. Demanding that you are allowed to covertly follow them, in disguise, every time they meet, is not a useful suggestion. However, asking him to include you more when the three of you meet might be a good idea. Perhaps you want him to phone you once when he's on a night out with her – just quickly, so you know he's still thinking about you. Don't expect him to pluck the perfect solution from thin air. He's far more likely to behave in the way you want him to if you let him know what that actually is.

And if he seems unwilling to make these little changes then you really need to be strong. Be honest with yourself about what you want and what you need to make you feel secure within a relationship. If this isn't being met then ask yourself how happy you will be if you compromise these expectations. And look carefully at his reluctance to alter his relationship with his ex in order to strengthen the relationship he has established with you. If all the signs point towards the overwhelming conclusion that he isn't quite over his last relationship, then remember that supporting him through a break up is the job for a therapist, not a girlfriend.

QUICK TIPS

1. A little jealousy is natural, don't beat yourself up for it. It would be more strange if you felt nothing at all about his relationship with the ex.

2. Try to be honest and open, not accusatory. Talk about your insecurities, don't make snappy demands.

3. If he isn't over the ex, don't be 'the one who helped him

realise he still loves her'. Just get out of it before it gets too messy.

Q We dated, and now he just wants to be friends. What can I do?

Here's what's happening and why

When two people begin dating it's highly probable that two completely different maps of where the relationship could be heading are in operation. So, to a guy, the woman he likes from work agreeing to a second date might be a great sign that she's definitely keen. Meanwhile the woman might be thinking that agreeing to dinner will give her a final chance to confirm her inkling that he really isn't 'the one'. The man's map is leading him to a spot marked 'X' where, instead of a pot of treasure, there is a ready-made serious relationship, while the woman's map is leading her far out of the jungle, back to being single, and away from aforementioned male. First impressions can be really helpful, but they can also be misleading. A few dates in, you may well find out that the 'charity work' he claimed to live for actually consists of buying *The Big Issue* once a month. You might discover that when he said his car was 'top of the range', he meant it was top of the range ten years ago. And you might well discover that the thick, lustrous hair you couldn't wait to run your fingers through is, in fact, a wig. Don't laugh, it happens . . .

And it's hard enough being the one who decides that this relationship isn't quite the one you've always dreamt of. Trying to find a tactful way of saying, 'thanks, but no thanks' can be really tough. But it's a million times worse if you're the one who does see a future for the relationship. So you've been dating for a few weeks or even a couple of months now. And they've been good dates. You've laughed at all his jokes, and not just because you forced yourself to in the name of being a good flirt. You've started seeing more of each other outside the safety of strictly-evening dates, so you've been for lunch and gone for romantic walks. You've started staying in together, getting out videos that you never pay much attention to. And you've started preceding stories about your friends with 'When you meet Jodie,' rather than 'If you ever meet my friends . . .' You now feel confident saying to other men, 'I'm sorry, but you can't take my number, I'm *seeing someone*.' You've stopped telling your friends not to call him 'your boyfriend' for fear of them jinxing it, because you're fairly sure that, soon, that's exactly what he will be. You've almost started to relax a little when he takes a whole day to return your calls. Almost. Not quite.

But then suddenly the phone calls die down a little. He wants to meet up less. And he doesn't seem to keen on attending that family barbecue with you anymore. Baffled, dazed and confused, you decide to confront him. After all, you've spent a lot of time with this man, you've passed on other men for this man. If he's going to crush all your dreams now, you want a damn good reason. 'You're a really great girl,' he explains as you fume silently at the other end of the phone, 'It's just that I think we'd be better off as friends. I'm not ready for a relationship yet. Can we keep in touch though? I still want us to hang out together.' Never before has the phrase 'great girl' sounded so bitterly insulting. Never before has an invitation to 'hang out' sounded so patronising. And never before has the desire to 'keep in touch' sounded so hysterically ridiculous. If he finishes off with 'It's not you, it's me,' then calmly step away from the phone, count to ten, and if you still need to explode with rage, then just do it.

And the initial fury isn't the worst part. Because during this phase, Phase One if you will, you just hate him. Phase One is all about how rubbish he, and probably any other male who happens to cross your path, is. It's Phase Two that can be really messy. Because it's then, once the dust has settled and the phone has been repaired from the smithereens you smashed it into, that you begin to blame yourself. Did I get too serious? Was I too pushy? Did I give too much? Did I give enough? And once we've exhausted all these options, we resort to our lowest point. Was I too ugly? Am I too fat? Was it that little mole on my bum that drove him away? When somebody tells us they'd rather be friends, no matter how much they try to convince us that it's 'nothing personal', it can feel like the most personal attack there is. So how do we deal with these feelings of rejection? And how do we begin to realise that, more often than not, it's not you and it *is* him?

Here's what to do about it

The cruel fact of the matter is that if somebody has decided that you're not quite 'the one', then there really is very little you can do about it. Sleeping with him won't change it. Buying him a shirt, a car or even an entire football team won't make him feel differently about you (although it might make you feel a little differently about your bank balance). And changing who you are won't make him change his mind. This might sound a little depressing, but facing up to this reality is the first part of the solution to this problem. Some relationships are destined to turn into the romances of the century, complete with hearts, flowers, spring weddings and 'happy ever afters'. Some – well, some aren't. They just aren't. Some are destined to turn into friendships. And more often than not you'll both realise this as the relationship progresses. If you realise that he's not right for you after a few weeks, then he's probably started to realise it too. But if this doesn't happen and you're left wondering what went wrong, there are a few steps you can take to help put the experience behind you, rather than dragging it into every potential relationship you encounter in the future.

First, you need to acknowledge that him cooling off is not a reflection of your own worth. Think back to times when you've known that things just haven't been right with a guy. Was it because you thought he was wholly unattractive? Was it because you thought he was a bad person? Was it because you thought he was completely unlovable? Probably not, or you wouldn't have been interested in him in the first place, would you? No, you probably just realised that, despite him being a complete catch, he simply wasn't right for you. And this is almost certainly how this guy sees you. His decision to go back to being friends speaks volumes about him and probably very little about you. Maybe he just isn't ready for a relationship. Maybe he's still dealing with issues from his last relationship. Maybe he's met somebody else and he just sees more of a future with her. Be realistic and acknowledge that there are a million different reasons for his reluctance to enter into a serious relationship with you, and 'You're too ugly' is only one of them, so the odds are against it.

Whatever you do, don't internalise the reason. Don't convince yourself that you are incapable of being loved or that you are desperately unattractive. Because if you do that you will carry these feelings far beyond the context of your current relationship. Sure, if there are lessons to be learned, then learn them. This relationship needn't be a complete waste of time. In fact, the only way it can be seen as a waste of anything is if you fail to learn from it. Use the demise of this relationship as a way of learning about yourself, and about relationships in general. But leave it at that. Don't become obsessed with what you did wrong. Or what it was that turned him off you. Because otherwise what you take away from the relationship could actually be very damaging. Far from being a temporary blip on the landscape of your love life, this little incident could turn into emotional baggage that you cart around from relationship to relationship. Carrying baggage like this will have an inevitable effect on your self-esteem and, consequently, on the way you conduct yourself in relationships. Try to leave the initial feelings of rejection and disappointment where you left the relationship, so that they don't have implications for the next man in your life.

QUICK TIPS

1. Things like deleting his text messages and taking his number out of your phone help.
2. Things like smashing up his car and bricking his windows don't.
3. Take away the lesson, not the rejection.

Q. Why have I started to feel trapped in this relationship?

Here's what's happening and why

When the initial intensity of a relationship begins to fade there are a number of things that go with it. It might be your ridiculously frantic sex life. It might be the twice-a-day visits from Interflora. It might be the weekly dinner dates in a restaurant that neither of you can really afford. But that's fine. Naturally these honeymoon-stage touches start to become less frequent as you settle into something more comfortable and more secure. However, occasionally, when the dust settles and the initial excitement wears off it can be the perfect time for us to take stock and realise that, actually, the relationship isn't exactly what we thought it was or was going to be. When your mind is no longer occupied by hearts, flowers and constant, all-consuming sex, it gives you a chance to realise that, in fact, all is not hearts and flowers. There is indeed trouble in paradise. If the relationship is not 100 per cent right for you, then it is at this stage, once you've moved out of the honeymoon period that you will begin to see it.

A great relationship can feel like a blessing, a treat, a dream. But on the other hand, a bad relationship can feel like a bind. Perhaps you feel like you're no longer free to socialise because of the hassle you get from 'him indoors' whenever you try to arrange a night out with the girls. After a while, leaving him to go to the pub feels like leaving your first-born child under the careful supervision of a babysitter named 'Olga the Childeater'. Or something along those lines. There are tantrums, sulks and a genuine look of panic as you try to subtly creep out of the door so as he won't notice. Then your night is punctuated by phone calls and text messages reminding you, as if you would ever have a chance to forget, that he still exists. Upon your return you are subjected to a police-style interrogation. Where did you go? Who did you see? What did you drink? How did you get home? Did you dance? Are you drunk? How many times did you go to the toilet? And so on. In fact, gradually, it becomes clear that it's far easier to simply stay at home. The hassle you get from the girls is nothing compared to the grief he'll give you if you miss your curfew and, horror of horrors, stay out past eleven o'clock.

Or maybe you're feeling trapped because, say, you feel like you have a duty to be there for your boyfriend because his mother is ill, and so you are excusing some of his behaviour even though you're not sure if you actually want to be in the relationship anyway. So you find yourself spending hours supporting him and his family, despite the fact that your efforts appear to be going entirely unnoticed by everyone involved. The relationship doesn't make you feel good any more – you wouldn't describe yourself as particularly happy – but you can't leave him now because it's just not 'the right time'. Guilt has you firmly pinned into a relationship that probably isn't right for you anyway.

Or maybe you hurtled into dating, mating and co-habiting at such a breakneck speed that now you feel out of your depth, drowning in a relationship that got far too serious far too quickly. You met, you went out for a few slap-up dinners and a few cosy drinks, and next thing you knew you were meeting family, merging bank accounts and moving in. And now that first flurry of excitement has died down somewhat, you're not in a fresh, exciting new relationship. You're practically married. After three months. Deep down you know that somehow the duration of your relationship does not warrant the depth of commitment you feel you have made, but how can you turn back now? Surely it's too late to say, 'Actually love, I'm not sure this is exactly what I want. Here's your engagement ring. Oh, and can you have your stuff out of here by tomorrow? Thanks.'

Whatever the reason behind the feeling that you have been taken hostage by your own relationship there is a common solution. Something needs to change. It might mean changing the hours you work to better suit the relationship or changing the number of times a week you sit in and watch TV together. Or it might mean changing something a little more drastic. Like who you're going out with.

Here's what to do about it

Ending the relationship might sound a little extreme. But if you feel utterly trapped, knowing when to say goodbye could be the key you need to get out. However, if you're not sure you're ready for that step, then you need to look closely at the reasons you feel so hedged in. They usually fall into two categories. The first are practical reasons. Perhaps you feel trapped because you've just moved into his flat and he won't let you move any of the furniture or make any changes or put your beloved Anne Geddes posters up (a baby in a flowerpot? Is there anything cuter?), for fear of blu-tack ruining his lovely aubergine paint. Or maybe you're earning more money than he is and he feels uncomfortable when you pay for all your evenings out, so you find you are becoming surgically joined to the sofa because he'd rather just stay in. Maybe you're looking for a place together but he refuses to live more than ten miles away from his family home, even though that means you relocating miles away from your mum and dad. All of these problems are rooted in practical issues and imposed on you by external forces. But their logistical nature means that they are also fairly easy to address. If you can pinpoint a factor or a behaviour that is causing you to feel unhappy within the relationship then it is far easier to target. This is where boundaries and expectations come into play again. You need to be honest with yourself about whether you can really live with the boundaries he has set. If he refuses to move out of a ten-mile radius of Mummy and Daddy, then make it clear to him that you also have some expectations of how close you want to be to your family home and clearly you both need to make some compromises. Likewise, if he hassles you every time you attempt to go out with the girls, then explain that you want to be able to see them once a week and that is what you need to do to be happy because it gives you time to enjoy and maintain friendships that are important to you. If you have begun to feel trapped because your expectations are not being met, then you need to clarify exactly what those expectations are and ensure that you are sticking to the boundaries it takes to make you happy.

But sometimes the reasons for your discomfort in the relationship are not so easy to pinpoint – sometimes they are more complex, linked to your emotions rather than the day-to-day functioning of your relationship. So maybe you feel trapped because you don't feel like the relationship is going anywhere or because you feel like he expects far more time and commitment than you are prepared to offer. Maybe the relationship just isn't making you feel good about yourself any more. A method therapists often use is to ask people not 'What do you feel?', but 'What do you *not* feel?' In this way you can look at the situation differently by asking yourself 'How is he *not* making me feel?' This will help you focus on what it is exactly you feel you are missing. So you might answer with 'He doesn't make me feel special. Or sexy. Or exciting. Or beautiful.' Look at what the opposite of what you're feeling is. Perhaps the solution is not as simple as asking him to let you go out more often. If, fundamentally, the relationship is making you feel bad about yourself rather than good, perhaps it's time to face up to the fact that you feel like the relationship isn't going anywhere because, in truth, it isn't.

QUICK TIPS

1. Be kind. You feeling trapped is not necessarily 'his fault', just something you need to work at together.
2. Address the problem before you reach breaking point.
3. Look at how often your relationship makes you happy and how often it makes you unhappy: it should help you answer a few other important questions.

Q. I don't find him attractive any more – why?

Here's what's happening and why

You still get a strange sensation when you think about the first time you saw him. The phrase 'butterflies in your tummy' sounds awfully clichéd, but you can't help thinking it's the only one that can really do justice to the way you felt when you first met him. Maybe it was the way his t-shirt was a little bit too tight and you could see his big, strong arms. Maybe it was his confident swagger. Maybe it was the way his eyes widened when you talked to him, so that you felt he was really, really listening. When we really, truly are attracted to someone it can be impossible to put our finger on exactly why. At first you thought it was 'wanting what you can't have' syndrome. Maybe you lusted after him like a crazed teenager because you assumed he was the property of some other lucky lady? But then, eventually, he became yours and you realised that, no, he actually was that attractive. Perhaps it was the allure of the unknown? Perhaps the grass just looked greener over at his end of the bar? Then you got to know him and realised that, up close and personal, he was still the sexiest man you had ever seen.

And then you moved on to a stage where you saw him at his worst. You saw him scratching his hairy belly, dribbling, half-dressed after he'd passed out in the living room after a night out with the boys. And somehow he still looked adorable. Suave? No. Sophisticated? No. But sexy? Hell, yes! Even when he had the flu, with a runny nose, a croaky voice and ridiculously exaggerated sense of the seriousness of his condition, you still wanted him. As long as he wiped his nose first. In fact, while you convinced yourself that if he saw you for too long without mascara he would probably walk out on you, he could have made himself as un-sexy and he would still be top of your list of heart-throbs.

So what changed? Suddenly you find yourself more

irritated than ignited by his presence. A slobbery kiss is more likely to be greeted with a 'Get off! You'll mess up my make-up!' than 'Oh yes! More, more!' And when you go to a party you're far too distracted by the Jude Law lookalike chatting to the hostess to notice that your man is wearing a new suit. Which he made the effort to go out and buy himself because you don't buy him clothes any more. In fact, the last present you bought him was an ice scraper so he could clear your car window in the mornings before you go to work. And that was six months ago. For his birthday . . .

You know you still love him, you know you do. You don't really want to be with anyone else, but you just wish you could have the same spark back. You want to be able to think 'wow' when he walks into a room, just like you used to. You want to tire of gawping at images of male models in too-tight briefs because you've got your own supermodel back home, just like you used to. You want to want him like you used to. So why don't you?

Here's what to do about it

Take a look at your man. And think about the man he was when you met him. Has he really changed that much? Probably not. You might have weaned him out of those awful shirts he used to wear. Perhaps he's gained a little bit of weight. Or lost a little bit of weight. Maybe you've managed to persuade him that only David Beckham can get away with a David Beckham hairdo, and he's shorn off the mullet. But essentially he still looks the same. So why doesn't he send the same tingles down your spine? Why don't you find him as attractive any more?

Well, the truth is that our attraction to somebody rarely has much to do with the way they look. Obviously, we can all appreciate a gorgeous face and a cracking pair of legs. But real sex appeal, real gritty attraction runs far deeper than this. Think back to when you were at school. There was probably one really cute guy with beautiful eyes, an athletic build and the best car. But he wasn't the one who everybody wanted to date, was he? No, that was his slightly naughtier, slightly cheekier mate, who had the best jokes and the smoothest chat-up lines. And if you're honest, when you met your boyfriend, although you might have noticed his not-bad physical attributes, the things that really drew you to him were things like his sense of confidence, the way he laughed at your jokes, the way he challenged you on some of your political beliefs, the way he held every door open for you and his genuine concern for your welfare. If you've stopped finding him as take-me-now sexy as you used to, it's probably because one of these things has changed, not because of that pimple on his chin.

Look at things that may have changed in his life that may have affected his behaviour. Perhaps he has lost his job? Or maybe he feels really under pressure at work? Maybe he senses that you don't find him as attractive any more and that is affecting his self-esteem? You need to talk to him about this one because it is something which can be changed. Don't think about this as a problem that he has to solve. Don't approach him with 'You're not sexy any more. Why?', unless you really want to send his self-esteem hurtling into an abyss of no return. Instead venture with 'I've noticed you don't seem quite yourself. Is there anything you want to talk about?' If he has gone through some changes in his life, then try and appreciate where he's coming from and how that would make you feel. Feeling devalued at work can be particularly hard for men because, traditionally, this is where their value to society lay. If they couldn't compete in the office, then they weren't valued particularly highly elsewhere. Reassure him that the way you feel about him has nothing to do with how successful he is in his career. Reassure him that you still value him very highly indeed. Perhaps he has put on a little weight, and he just needs reassurance from you that it wasn't a toned, tight tummy that made you fall in love, it was everything else that came with it. Whatever the reason, if his confidence has taken a knock somewhere along the line, then you can play a major part in rebuilding it.

Perhaps the relationship has gone through some kind of change and this has affected the way you feel about him. You need to address this with him. Finding each other attractive, or not as the case may be, is an issue that needs to be addressed by both of you. It is impossible to solve single-handedly, so communication is key.

NEVER GIVE UP ON A GOOD THING . . . SURVIVING THE MIDDLE STAGE

This stage is about learning to live with the relationship you have built between you. You've laid the foundations, you've argued over the décor and now it's time to live with your choices. That doesn't mean that if the relationship starts failing to meet your expectations or if you suddenly feel your boundaries are not being respected that you can't walk away. It just means that now you have made far more of a commitment than a date in a fancy wine bar to this person, and you are likely to work a little harder to keep things going. If the sex begins to dwindle, you're more likely to work at it. If you begin to have the same old arguments, you're more likely to try and break the cycle.

The middle stage is a difficult one to define, because although you have certainly settled into a far more comfortable, more constant rhythm, this doesn't mean that the stage where you are finding out about the other person has come to an end. Because that never really comes to an end, you can never know everything there is to know. But you are a little better equipped than you are during the first few months to make judgements on his behaviour within the relationship. So if he starts staying at his place after months of staying at yours with you, you are in a far better position to look into the reasons for this. However, you're not quite at that stage yet where you have encountered every new hurdle that you're likely to encounter either, so there is still a great wealth of the unknown open to you. Your progression into this next, rock-solid stage in your relationship depends on your ability to adapt, to learn and to negotiate your way through this tricky middle stage.

Part Three

HAPPILY EVER AFTER

or happily ever after
(but not with him . . .)

HOME AND DRY, MAYBE . . .

Once we've navigated through the minefields of blind dating, double dating and downright disaster dating, through the trials of commitment making, parent meeting and friend merging, believe it or not there's still a whole new stage to move on to. And a key feature of this stage is decision making. After you've worked through the beginning of your relationship and then the middle, it doesn't necessarily mean that the next logical step is the end. But it might be. You might have been right when you told all your friends 3.3 seconds after seeing him in the supermarket that he was the man you would spend the rest of your life with. Perhaps kids, a jazzy 4x4 and a beautiful family home are just round the corner. But just as likely as this turn of events is the realisation that perhaps he isn't the one. And perhaps a sexy, convertible two-seater and a stylish one-bedroom apartment overlooking the Thames is next on your agenda . . .

This last section is about the fork in the road. It's about collecting your thoughts, your belongings and deciding whether you need to take them far, far away or install them neatly into the lovely new life you share with him. It's about the decision between claiming back your CDs or integrating them meticulously into his collection – alphabetically, of course. It's about realising that you've stopped searching for the fairytale because you've found it. Or realising that you still want the fairytale and when you picture the wedding, the dress, the church and everything else, you just don't see his face at the top of the aisle. You don't necessarily see anyone else, in fact at the moment your future soon-to-be husband is more of a blurry apparition, but you just don't see him. Perhaps you already love the old man that he will mature into, because you know he will be perfect for the older lady that you will become. Or perhaps the thought of him with grey hair and minus his devastatingly tight buttocks bores you. If you've stopped noticing other men, it's a sign. If you stop noticing *him* the moment a half-decent human of the male variety walks into the room, then that's a sign too.

Although this stage is about making life-changing progressions, that doesn't mean that you should go into anything blindly. Yes, the road might be forking just ahead of you. But the road signs along the way will help you pick the right route. This section of *The Man Manual* will help you to identify a few of these signs. Should you be saying, 'I do' or 'No thanks, see you around'? Is he 'the one'? Are you even ready for 'the one'? And if the answer to the last two questions is 'no', then how do you move on with maximum dignity and minimum heartache? If the answer is a smug, loved-up 'yes', then how do you ensure that paradise remains trouble free? How do you stop love's young dream turning into your worst nightmare? Part Three is about moving forward, moving in and moving on.

DVDS, BIG JUMPERS AND OTHER THINGS TO TAKE FROM A RELATIONSHIP

Right, let's start with the end as it were. If you decide that, despite all the good points, what you have isn't quite right, you need to make a tough decision. For you, the last big stage of your relationship might just be when you say goodbye. The beginning stages of relationships are all frivolous sex, tummy butterflies and six new outfits for every single date (just so you cover every possibility, obviously . . .). Big, life-changing decisions don't come into it. Who cares if he wants kids and you don't when you're only popping to the cinema to see the new Brad Pitt film? So what if he's only prepared to marry someone who shares his religion, when you're still at the stage where sharing a toothbrush is a step too far? It's only when we move further into a relationship that these issues become relevant. So you might realise that, after six months, he's great fun, he's charming, debonair, courteous, in fact he's everything you've ever wanted in a man, but ultimately he's not ever going to be ready to make the kind of commitment *you* were gagging for four months ago. It might be a gradual thing. Yeah, you've met his parents, but they keep calling you Sara . . . (Which wouldn't be *that* disconcerting, but your name is actually Nikki.) Perhaps you've bought a pet together, but he keeps calling it 'your bloody cat' whenever it snags his favourite trousers. And then there's that conversation you had the other day, when he insisted 'hypothetically' that if you were ever to split up, you could, of course, keep little Snooty. No questions asked. Maybe he keeps hiding those *Sandals* holiday brochures as sneakily as you keep placing them strategically in his eye line on the coffee table. Maybe a few months of these types of signals add up to the heart-wrenching discovery that he might be your 'one', but perhaps you're not his. Or perhaps you are but he isn't ready to find 'the one' just yet, which, in real terms, equates to the same outcome.

Or maybe your discovery that the two of you aren't quite as close to running off into the sunset as you had previously thought is more of a short, sharp shock. Like capitalising on that leap year, buying a ring, risking that gorgeous Joseph skirt to get down on one knee, popping the question – and getting turned down. Or coming home one day and finding a Dear John (or Dear Jo, to be precise) letter where you were pretty sure there was going to be a beautifully-cooked lasagne and a cool glass of chardonnay.

Then again, perhaps it's not him who isn't ready to commit. Maybe you've been feeling increasingly trapped by his fascination with weddings, baby names and that funky three-wheeled pushchair that Jude Law has got. Perhaps overhearing his party small talk to strangers brings you out in a cold sweat. Because he isn't talking about how fluffy the vol-au-vent cases are or how fantastic the champagne is. He's talking about how he and his girlfriend 'will probably move away from the area in the next couple of years, certainly before the children start walking'. Children? Moving? News to you! And everybody knows that no news is good news. Hearing the next five, ten, fifteen years of your life described to a complete stranger by a man who has just recently moved from 'date' to 'boyfriend', is very, very bad news.

Often, realising that the two of you are moving at an

entirely different pace to one another means you need more than a little catch-up period while you stop knitting baby booties long enough for him to come around to the idea of a commitment more solid than leaving his after-shave at your flat. Our thoughts on the speed at which a relationship should be moving are not just a reflection of our relationship boundaries. Sometimes they are a reflection of the specific relationship you're in right now. So, maybe you *do* see yourself with 2.4 children and a re-assuringly hefty mortgage. But you've just never seen your current relationship like that. You do want to find the man you can do all those things with, but you're just not sure that this man is *the* man.

And lots of women have suffered the situation in reverse. Your wonderful, if elusive, boyfriend hits you one day with the revelation that he's just 'not ready for a relationship'. Fine. Well, OK, so it's not 'fine', but you're a big girl now, you'll learn to live with it. He thinks you're 'great' and 'just the type of woman he wants to settle down with – not yet, but one day'. So you split, and you move on, while secretly harbouring the suspicion that once his philander-ing days are dead and gone, he will return to you, ready for a top hat, tails and Mothercare. Of course, these suspicions are shaken a little when you hear, by way of a gossipy hairdresser or the office bitch, that he is now engaged. 'She probably conned him into it', you reason with yourself, 'He'll get scared soon and make a run for it.' Well, that's until months later when you bump into him shopping with aforementioned fiancée. And to add insult to heartfelt injury, he's carrying one of those fluffy baby carriers. And just to top it all off . . . there's a baby in it! So while your mouth is saying, 'He's beautiful. He looks just like you – you must be so proud . . .' your mind is thinking, 'But, you said you weren't ready for a relationship. What the bloody hell is wrong with me?'

And here, ladies, lies your introduction to the fact that, sometimes, just like 'I'll call' means 'I'll never call', 'I'm not ready for a relationship' means 'I'm not ready for a relationship . . . with you.' Often the realisation that you are working at entirely different speeds is the wake-up call you need to appreciate that perhaps this relationship isn't the one that will make it up the aisle.

And that doesn't mean that the past however many weeks or months have been a complete waste of everybody's time. It doesn't mean you have to buy a magic time capsule and wish, wish, wish yourself back to the three minutes before you uttered the fatal words, 'Yes, sure, I'd *love* to go for a drink.' Because the only way a relationship can be a waste of time is if you let it be. If you fail to take anything away from the time you spend with somebody, then of course it can appear to be a big fat black hole in your dating history. But look at it like this. How many people do you know who stumbled into the perfect relationship at the age of eighteen and have stayed in love forever after? Probably not many. So the odds are that you will have more than one meaningful relationship in your life (not counting that time you 'married' Sammy in the sandpit at primary school).

Don't go thinking that the sole purpose of each relationship is to find the one man who will love you, want you and keep you satisfied for the rest of your life. Till death do you part. Because the rules of probability mean that most men will not fit these requirements. That doesn't mean you can't learn fundamental stuff about life, love and yourself from them. So your first boyfriend might have taught you that if a man really loves you, he doesn't mind waiting for sex. Your next boyfriend might have helped you learn to trust a man as comprehensively as you trust your friends, or even yourself.

Perhaps you realise that it's time to move on not because one of you isn't ready for the commitment you appear to be heading towards, but because your boundaries have been crossed. Perhaps your man can't accept that time with your girlfriends is essential to you, and that only seeing them on birthdays ending in 'o' is not enough. Or maybe you've come to the painful conclusion that phone numbers in his jacket pocket and lipstick (well, the obvious gloss of a Lancome Juicy Tube) on his collar are not just old-fashioned clichés. And that those crumpled knickers you keep finding under the pillows probably *aren't* 'a surprise present'! Even if the end of your relationship isn't quite amicable enough to make Hugh and Liz look like bitter enemies, there are still valuable lessons you can take with you. Bad relationships help us learn too. So, one man could teach you that you're happiest when you *don't* compromise your boundaries. Another boyfriend could show you that unless you demand respect you don't often get it.

The point is, starting a new relationship is about embracing a new experience, and grabbing an opportunity to learn more about yourself and life in general. Let it last as long as it will, but always think of it as a learning experience. Clearly, there is a negative side to any relationship ending, but try to see the positive that also comes out of the situation. If anything, when you end a relationship with somebody else it should improve the relationship you have with yourself, because you know that little bit more about who you are and what you want. As long as you take that knowledge and apply it in the future, you've lost nothing. If the initial bond between you and your man turns into a life-long commitment, then obviously you've gained something wonderful. But if it doesn't, make sure you take what you can from it.

BREAKING UP IS HARD TO DO . . .

Now, of course, this all sounds a little easier said than done. When your heart is bruised, battered and you feel like emotional roadkill, your focus isn't necessarily on the life-long love lessons you can take from your latest romantic disaster. Physical violence? Yes. Brutal acts of vandalism? Yes. But elevating yourself above the crisis and enriching yourself with a valuable lesson? Nope. Perhaps looking at the relationship from an analytical point of view is something that comes later for you, and that's fine. But to minimise the hurt you feel right at the beginning, it's important that you take a few things into consideration immediately.

Remember that it takes two people to make a relationship work and only one to ensure it doesn't. For all your efforts, if he's decided that he's just not up for the relationship, then it won't happen and it really is as simple as that. You can't keep a relationship going by yourself, no matter how convinced you are that he's the one for you. And the problem is that men are far less comfortable explaining that they aren't happy than women.

This all goes back to emotional literacy and the historical legacy of women being 'talkers' and men being 'do-ers'. So when we feel unhappy or unfulfilled, talking about it to our friends, our mothers or even a stranger in the queue at Mango is almost second nature. We are far more adept at identifying problems and speculating about what might be causing them. (Occasionally to a point of paranoia. Sure, sometimes that extra half hour he spends at the pub *does* mean that the relationship is going down the pan, but mostly it just means he wants to spend an extra half hour down the pub). Men, on the other hand, do not feel the immediate urge to talk to their mates, their family and probably, strangely, least of all you, about their relationship fears.

Take a typical trip to the hairdressers. So what if this is the first time Vikki has done your hair? She already knows what your man is called, how long you've been together and what you're getting him for Christmas, so she's already one up on him. By the end of your cut and blow dry, you're wishing each other well and promising to update each other in, well, precisely six weeks. Now look at his visit to the barbers. The conversation is unlikely to delve beneath the surface of the latest premiership results. Your man and his stylist will not, absolutely will not, begin talking about their relationship concerns. There might be a passing reference to 'the missus', but that's only because he's moaning that you taped over his *Match of the Day* video collection.

This discomfort with talking about personal feelings explains why the answer to 'What are you thinking about?' is so often 'Nothing'. And it also explains why when a relationship is over in his mind, you might just be the last one to know. When you end a relationship you probably feel that you've given him more than adequate notice. You've discussed the problems as and when they've arisen, and upon realising that your relationship doesn't have a future you've explained this to him. Men tend to fear this type of confrontation. So it seems far easier to just call you less or stand you up or cheat on you so you get the general idea.

Poll after poll, study after study, consistently reveals that men are far more likely to cheat than women. One way to understand cheating is as a classic example of a man demonstrating how he feels through actions, rather than through conversation. Which might work best for him, but it does nothing for the woman in the situation. His lack of communication means that she is left in the dark, often waiting for the verbal negotiation that she feels more comfortable with. Lack of communication is the chief reason break-ups comes as a surprise. And it's not a nice surprise.

This part of *The Man Manual* talks about looking for those signs that mean he's thinking more along the lines of 'goodbye' than 'I do'. Basically, if you're tolerating behaviour that makes you unhappy, you need to address it as soon as you can. It might be a sign that he's just not the man you thought he was, or it might be a sign that he's looking for a way out. Either way, putting up with repeat infringements of your boundaries will not make you happy. But if you feel the relationship is working perfectly and he still isn't happy, then the rather depressing fact of it is that there isn't much you can do. This goes back to the idea that it takes two to maintain a relationship and only one to destroy it. So, one of the first steps is accepting that if one of you is not committing fully to the relationship, it is unlikely to have a serious future.

The second really important step you need to make, if the demise of the relationship is not exactly what you had been hoping for, is to acknowledge that the situation is not a brutal reflection of your own worth. If you get to the stage of a relationship where words like 'cohabitation', 'engagement' and 'joint mortgage' begin to be thrown around, and he decides he isn't ready for any of it, then you need to accept that this is as much to do with him as it is to do with you. Think about break-ups your friends have been through. Now, when they've sat there wailing, 'It's because I'm fat/ugly/useless in bed/too poor/too rich/too keen/not keen enough' [delete as applicable], what has your reaction been? 'Yeah, you're right, I'd diet, have a face lift and get my boobs lifted six inches if I were you.'? No, of course not. Because when you're not a main player in the drama it's far easier to look at it rationally. So you tell her, 'Don't be ridiculous, he wasn't right for you, he's not ready for the type of relationship you want right now.' So, if you're the victim of an unwanted relationship discontinuation, then be your own best friend. Look in on the situation from an impartial bystander's point of view. This should help you to see that your boyfriend's (or ex-boyfriend's) decision to end things probably has far more to do with where he is emotionally, than that little spare tyre you've been grudgingly carrying around lately.

Or perhaps your ending doesn't feature your heart being drop kicked off a multistorey and trampled on at the bottom. Maybe *you're* the one doing the dumping. Sure, being broken up with is ghastly, but anyone who has tried to 'exit stage left' from a relationship with a perfectly good man will tell you that, sometimes, getting dumped yourself seems preferable. Sometimes it occurs to you over a long period. Sometimes, it comes to you as a short, sharp shock. But when you know it's over, you know it's over.

There is no uncertainty, there is no doubt, when you know, you know. And once you've established that this one isn't 'the one', then every second seems like a waste of time. Every moment is a moment you could be spending looking for the man who is right for you or just catching up with some quality single-girl time. If you've decided that the relationship is over because you feel trapped, then those days, weeks (or months if you're a real wimp) between making the decision and ending it will feel like a holiday on Alcatraz. Because feeling slightly trapped in a relationship you are basically happy with is nothing compared to feeling trapped in a relationship that you know you need to break free from.

Like so many dilemmas we face in life, the answer really is just to be clear and honest. And as soon as possible. You don't protect anybody by dragging out a unsuccessful relationship. If you're ready to leave the party, then go while the DJ's still playing and the disco lights are still on. Don't wait until the music stops and the cold light of day exposes the real damage and destruction. If you've just fallen out of love with your man, then end it now before you begin to lose all affection for each other at all or, worse, drive yourself to a point of hatred where you can't bear to be in the same postal area let alone room as one another.

The more decisive and efficient you are about ending things before you hit the dregs of your relationship, the better chance you have of salvaging a healthy friendship at a later date. The longer you leave it, the more opportunity there is for bitterness and anger to take over your relationship. So, if you're going to do it, do it now.

And don't lie. Don't say, 'It's not you, it's me', because

clearly it is him a little bit. It must be, or you wouldn't want to end the relationship. Don't say, 'I just need some space', when you're thinking in years and lifetimes rather than popping out to the shops for a couple of hours. Don't say, 'we can give it time', when in two weeks you see yourself living it up as a single girl, preferably on a beach full of Brad Pitt lookalikes, not recontemplating the pros and cons of forever together with a man you don't want to be with. Be strong and unambiguous. If you're certain that the relationship won't go anywhere, then say that. If you've fallen out of love with him, then that's what he needs to hear. Ultimately, being lied to doesn't help anybody.

And a note on 'being friends'. It's understandable that you want to maintain contact with this person, particularly if your relationship was very serious. After all, when we are in relationships we make all kinds of links and commitments, to his family, to his friends, to his lifestyle in general. We also make emotional links. We can get used to depending on our partners, not just for the support that comes through being a lover but also as a friend.

Unfortunately, downgrading your relationship from 'partners' to 'friends' overnight is virtually impossible, because it requires a complete change in who you are with each other and how you relate to one another. Think about what the word 'friend' means to you. Someone you trust? Someone you have fun with? Someone you share your love-life details with? Well, how can you talk to him about your love-life woes, when he *is* your love-life woe? And maybe you've got over the break-up, but that doesn't mean he wants to hear about the hot man you picked up in the coffee shop. This doesn't mean that you can't revisit the situation and consider establishing a friendship once the dust has settled.

It just means that two days after you dump him you shouldn't be ringing him telling him you've found 'the best sex of your life'!

So whether you're the dumper or the dumpee it helps to make a mental checklist of things you need to pack up in your suitcase when you leave a relationship. Make sure you take with you: any lessons you have learned about love, life and your behaviour in relationships; your self-esteem: memories of times when the relationship was right; your toothbrush; and any DVDs that you're sure he won't notice . . . Things to leave behind include: blame, guilt and that manky pink razor in the bathroom . . .

Now, of course, breaking up is just one possible ending for your relationship. It's a bit like when *EastEnders* or *Friends* have a cracking climax episode or season finale, and they film loads of different endings to throw us all off the scent. The next episode in your mini-drama will be thrilling and enlightening, but you'll only know which ending it is once you get there. And one of you packing your bags and hitting the road is one possible ending, sure. But, if you're both dedicated to the relationship and ready for the commitment it requires, you could well find yourself starring in a series that could run and run. So how do we know when it's time to stop channel hopping and settle into our own love story?

COMPLETENESS FIRST, THEN COMMITMENT

Commitment really is one of those things that can be completely lost on us unless we're ready for it. And there is a curious irony to when this occurs, exactly. Because the times when we are curled up under the duvet feeling (a) fat, (b) useless or (c) miserable after another (a) rubbish day at work, (b) painfully yawn-inducing date or (c) disastrous shopping trip, are the times when we most feel like we need someone else. We need someone else to make us feel loved. We need someone else to make us feel valid. We need someone else to make us feel confident. We need the validation of a significant other to prove that we aren't all the things our self-esteem is telling us we are. But relationships shouldn't be about need. In fact, on the contrary, the healthiest time to enter into a commitment with someone else is when you don't 'need' to do it at all. When you're happy within yourself. When you feel content and complete. When a relationship is going to be the cherry on top of the ice bun, not part of your staple diet.

Even at this late stage of the proceedings – in fact, especially at this stage – everything we talked about in relation to not looking for another half to complete us holds good. We need to take responsibility for our own 'completeness'. We really aren't ready to be somebody else's other half until we are whole ourselves.

But what exactly does it mean, being 'whole ourselves'? Well, by the time we get to this stage, hopefully it means we know who we are and we have faith in what we believe. It means we know what we will accept and what we can't tolerate. It means we can identify, acknowledge and live according to our strengths and weaknesses. It means we feel good about our thighs, hair, skin and height without needing somebody else to tell us to feel good about them.

The boundaries and expectations we talked about in the first section of *The Man Manual*, on those initial dating dilemmas, are just as important in the latter stages of your relationship. Just as you need to be clear on your boundaries about things such as when you will sleep with someone and when they can meet your parents, boundaries come into play over things like when you will move in with somebody and the kind of behaviour you expect from them if you do. We're ready for commitment when we know what we want from it. And when we feel confident enough to express these expectations to somebody else. And stick by them. Don't draw up a contract with convoluted clauses and a sixty-five-page appendix; just make it clear that you need certain things to make you happy. And that's just the way it is.

KEEP WORKING AT IT

So let's say you have managed to snag that man who does appreciate boundaries. He does understand and respect the type of relationship you want to build with him. You don't depend on him, but you could if you needed to. You don't desperately need him, but you love him being around. And you know he feels the same way. So that's it, right? Surely, you can close *The Man Manual* now? You can kick it under your bed, or pop it in the post to your single friend, who has recently turned into Bridget Jones's sadder, lonelier, more neurotic twin . . . Surely? After all, finding the right man is the hard bit. You're out of the dating jungle, back to civilisation. You've found your Tarzan, brushed him up a bit and put him in a Prada suit (leopard print is sooo circa 1999!). You've done the hard work, can't you just relax a little now?

Well, not really. Sorry ladies. Of course you can enjoy

the comfort and security that a loving relationship can bring. Of course you should have faith, confidence and trust in your partner. Of course you can feel a little smug about how happy your man makes you. Of course, of course, of course. Otherwise, what's the point in all of the heartbreak we put ourselves through to get to this stage? But it's important to acknowledge that shifting your boyfriend from 'date' to 'serious boyfriend', or from 'serious boyfriend' to 'live-in lover' does not mean that your work here is done. Or that *The Man Manual* can begin its new career as a doorstop. Oh no. Because in the 'top twenty' of things that will kill your relationship, 'complacency' is definitely in the top three (right behind infidelity and the evil that is the PlayStation). Happily ever after doesn't mean 'job done'. It means that you're in a relationship that you will work at because it's definitely worth working at.

And it's called 'work' for a reason. Because keeping a relationship strong is not exactly a walk in the park. Unless your average walk in the park involves reaffirming trust, confidence, support and sensuality. Thought not. You owe it to yourself, your man and your relationship to keep the promises you made when everything was new. So if you always used to set aside Sunday mornings for lazy 'together time', then keep it up. If you used to promise each other you would go out for dinner at least once a week, then why change now? If he used to be your main priority, why should he slip down the list just because you've been together for a while? 'But he *knows* I love him now!' isn't good enough. The process of crystallisation we mentioned in the middle stage of *The Man Manual* means that as the initial excitement of new love dies down, you should put even more effort in rather than just going with the flow.

And as well as making sure that your partner still feels special, you need to ensure that *you* still feel special too. This means that when insecurities and worries come up you can talk to your partner about them. If the relationship isn't making you feel great about yourself, it doesn't necessarily mean that you should immediately consider your boundaries violated and your expectations squandered. So often the insecurities, dilemmas and fears we face in our relationships are products of our own doing, and not necessarily his fault.

So if you are, let's say, convinced – absolutely convinced – that your man is having an affair with his ex-girlfriend, this suspicion could just be a result of your own insecurities rather than a reflection of the truth. Perhaps you're feeling a little down and you can't see why your wonderful boyfriend would want to be with you, so your imagination tells you he doesn't. Now, of course, your boyfriend's friendship with his ex might be just that: friendship. But the only way to distinguish between a real-life affair and one created by your own insecurities is to talk to him about it.

Communication is really, really important in the more serious stages of a relationship, because insecurities can so often be dispelled by a single conversation. If you just need to hear 'I love you' more, then that's fine. If you just need to have a good old night out together, to re-affirm the fun you have when it's just the two of you, then do it. The only way you will come up with a joint solution to these relationship problems is to address them together. And the only way to keep a relationship going is to keep talking to each other.

And just as one of the secrets of a happy, enduring relationship is to do things together, another one is doing things apart. Because as strongly as your joint personality evolves, you need to ensure that your individual personalities are still very much intact. If you really want longevity, you need to continue to grow as a person within a relationship, not just as a couple. This means that you can both keep bringing new things to your time together, and it also means you avoid the 'stuck-in-a-rut' feeling that can be a common feature at this stage of things. So keep doing the things you always did, the things you loved long before you started loving him, because these are probably the things that make you happy, outside of your relationship. This just goes back to staying true to who you are. You're far more capable of making somebody else happy if you are happy yourself.

So, keeping a relationship going involves a little work. It might not be the easy breeze through you had been expecting. But that doesn't mean it can't be fun. In fact, it *has* to be fun or there's no point. So, sure, work hard at your relationship. But make sure you are still spontaneous, impulsive, carefree and all those other things that seem to come so easily when we're just starting out. Keep letting go, and keep trying new things. Yes, you need to give your relationship some solid foundations, but you also need to make sure you keep it alive.

WHAT'S NEXT?

This section of *The Man Manual* is ultimately about decisions. And not decisions like: 'brown or white bread?', 'cinema or pub?', 'bomber or bolero jacket?' Decisions that will change your life. Decisions that dictate who you are, who you will be, who you are with and who you will be with. If there is anything that distinguishes this stage of a relationship from the beginning and middle stages it's the magnitude of the decisions you make. Because, as time goes on, you invest more and more in relationships. And this can be a good thing or a bad thing. If you are investing more in a healthy, happy relationship, the rewards are brilliant. If, however, you are investing time and effort in a relationship that has no future, the results can be pretty devastating. Identifying which situation you're in is the first step. Making decisions according to that is the next. Whether you see your relationship lasting to infinity and beyond, or just beyond the time it takes you to pack your stuff and leave, the most important thing is that you remain true to yourself. Make sure that the decisions you make are best for *you*. Be your own best friend and the rest will take care of itself.

Q. How can I find out if he loves me without scaring him away?

Here's what's happening and why

Those three *little* words are a big deal aren't they? It doesn't matter that you've made a firm commitment to each other and spend every spare minute gazing into each other's puppy-dog eyes. Sure, he tells you he thinks you're great all the time. He says you're beautiful. He says you're sexy (even the day *before* your bikini-wax appointment, when you're fairly sure you're not *that* sexy). He says he's proud to be with you. He even says you're 'his world'. Which is all lovely and wonderful and blah, blah, blah. But who cares about all that stuff? You're waiting for the big one. The final frontier. 'I like you lots' is nice, but not when you want to hear the other I-word. And it's got to be said properly too. 'I love you to bits' won't cut it. Neither will 'That's why I love you!' (usually in a patronising tone after you say something silly). No, you're looking for a pure, unadulterated, clear-cut, 'I love you'.

That's all, just three little words. How hard can it be? He gets in from the pub, slouches in an armchair, cracks open yet another beer and declares, 'Oh yeah, I had a great night. I love Jonesy, he's like my brother.' He'll quite happily describe his *car* as the 'love of his life' – in fact you're fairly sure that he's uttered the three magic words to the heap of metal on the driveway when you've been out of earshot. He 'loves' golf. He 'loves' Sunday roasts. He 'loves' Paul Smith ties. He 'loves' Franz Ferdinand's new album. But when it comes to you, the I-word seems a little harder to utter.

And how come you haven't said it either? Well, half the problem is that ridiculous dating guides, past experience and ill-informed advice from our well-intentioned mates has taught us that being the first to say, 'I love you' is a crime on a level with boiling his pet bunny. Because the worst thing that could happen, if you can bear to think about it, is that your declaration of love may well be met by a deathly silence, or worse: 'thanks!' So, you're sure that he really is 'the one'. You've never felt this way before, and you've come to the point where you realise that every other 'love' you've ever had before has, in fact, just been a warm up for the main event. And, understandably, you want to tell him this. But the 'love' word just has an extra dimension that takes it way beyond 'like', 'adore' and even 'worship'. So, you hold back. And sit patiently. Moaning incessantly to your friends, family and any other poor soul who hangs around long enough to hear your tale of woe.

So why hasn't he said those three little words? The key is to realise that men are so different to women. And, to be honest, if you haven't realised that by this stage of *The Manual*, you really haven't been paying attention! They really don't feel as comfortable talking about their feelings as women do. And as feelings go, love is a pretty big one to deal with. Men are far more about actions than women; they always have been. So perhaps the equivalent of you saying, 'I love you,' is him washing your car. Maybe that breakfast in bed is his 'I love you'. He could just be behaving like a typical man and curtailing the expression of emotions, verbally at least. Also, to some people, certain phrases and emotions mean different things. If he never heard 'I love you' as a child, it is understandable that it doesn't quite come easily to him as an adult. If his last girlfriend used 'I love you' as a tool to manipulate him or emotionally blackmail him, then perhaps the phrase holds certain negative connotations for him. There are a number of reasons why people just don't say, 'I love you', and his lack of verbal 'loving' doesn't mean that he isn't showing it in other ways.

But, if you really feel that you should be hearing those three little words (OK scratch that, they're not 'little' words, they're massive, and they would mean the world to you), then there are a few things you can do to encourage him to express this emotion.

Here's what to do about it

Well, the first tip is a simple but slightly scary one. Just say it first. Forget the rubbish about power, playing hard to get and basically manipulating your relationship. If you feel it, be honest. You're not in the school playground now, and your declaration of love will not be met with, 'Do you? Ugh yuck, that's disgusting! I hate girls! I'm off!' (If it is, stop dating him immediately.) Be a grown up and have the courage to let him know how you feel and stand by it. Don't wait till that crucial moment when you're 100 per cent sure he's going to say it back, because that's not a valid reason for saying, 'I love you'. Think of all those moments when you've wanted to say it – after great sex, after he shouted at that man in the car park who nicked your space, when he first cried in front of you – and promise that you'll grab the next one that comes along. Just be honest, and make it simple. After you've said it, move on. If he replies with 'I love you too', then great. If he doesn't, fine. Move on, talk about something else. Don't sit there with baited breath, a quizzical expression and an elbow digging his ribs while you do your very best subtle wink at him.

Try not to ask him 'Do you love me?' Trust him to come to you and say it in his own time. Do you really want to hear it if you have had to harass it out of him? Honestly, a forced, staged, unnatural 'Er . . . yeah . . . I do love you . . . er . . . I suppose' is actually worse than a silence. Really. Don't force it. It's far braver and more effective to just take the initiative and tell him you love him rather than try and sledgehammer it out of him first. Because you might get it out of him that first time, but you'll never get a spontaneous 'I love you', and that sledgehammer might wear out . . .

At first, it's fine if he doesn't reply with a ditto. He might just not feel ready yet. But if you get to a point where you said, 'I love you' months ago, and he still hasn't uttered the magic words, then you could have more of a problem on your hands. If the relationship is still happy and healthy, and he seems as into you as ever, then you might just need to accept that he's never going to be a big 'I love you' man. This might be something you can deal with, but you need to be very clear about whether his lack of verbal emotion matters to you or not. If you want to hear 'I love you' every day and you're hearing it, well, never, then maybe you need to accept that as much as you love him, this man will never make you completely happy. It's only four letters, but, if they matter that much to you and you're never going to hear them, they could spell the end.

QUICK TIPS

1. Be brave. Say it first.
2. Don't give to receive. Don't say, 'I love you,' just to hear 'I love you'.
3. Start thinking of a quick conversation topic to begin on immediately after you've done the deed, in case of deathly silence.

Q. Why does moving in together scare him so much?

Here's what's happening and why

Some days it's like he lives at yours anyway. You wake up, he's there. You get out of the shower, he's there. You get back from work, he's there. You make dinner, he's *definitely* there. And then, just before you turn off your bedside lamp, you glance over your shoulder and he's there. OK, he's snoring, dribbling and altogether *not* at his most attractive, but he's there nevertheless. And you're not complaining. You quite like the gruff, rhythmic sniffling and snuffling coming from the pillow next to you every night. It's a quite a nice feeling when you get in and immediately trip over one of his trainers, because it means that he's already there. And it's even nicer when he's tidied up a bit too. Yes, admittedly, his idea of 'tidying up' is putting his takeaway container in the bin and emptying the toaster of the burnt bit he forgot about earlier. (But in these circumstances you have to be thankful for small mercies, and they do say it's the thought that counts.)

If you're honest with yourself, when he's not around it feels a little strange. You've just got so used to having him there. And you're sick of staying at his and having to face a hectic rush to get ready for work when you realise you've left everything you need at home. OK, so you can handle borrowing his toothbrush and shampoo, but, strangely, he never seems to have a spare pair of ten-denier stockings or any tampons. The drawer you allocated him when he first started to stay at yours has expanded to incorporate your bedroom, your living room and, well, pretty much your whole flat. You've come to that point where moving in together just makes sense. Logistically and emotionally.

But try telling him that. Have you asked him to set light to his football memorabilia collection? No. Have you asked him to hand his firstborn to the devil? No. Have you told him that his local is about to be converted into a chess club? No. So, why on earth has he come out in a cold sweat, eyes wide and palms skyward? How on earth can the suggestion that you live together evoke such panic when you're practically doing it anyway? He spends thirty hours a day mooching around your flat (you're not sure how it's possible, but he does), so why can't he just mooch around a place that belongs to both of you instead? What difference does it make? Between the two of you, there's a double bed empty every night because you're always together at his or yours. So why not economise and just have one bed? Your car practically drives to his on autopilot, you do the journey so often. So why not cut out the travel time and *always* be at his place because it's your place too? Initially, his distress at the very suggestion is slightly amusing, then it becomes a little irritating, finally culminating in kick-the-coffee-table, pull-your-hair-out frustration. You're pretty much ready to share your life with this man, and he can't even share a living room.

It's really easy to assume that his reluctance to play house is a reflection of the way he feels about you. If you're ready for the next step and he's dragging his heels, it can look like he just doesn't take the relationship as seriously as you do. At any stage of a relationship it's hard when you feel like you're giving more than you're receiving. And the results can be dramatic. Because at first 'moving in together' is a casual suggestion. The concept begins life as an innocent fledgling idea. It would make life a bit easier and it would give you an excuse to hit the Habitat catalogue – but it's not a life or death issue. Until he responds. Because he doesn't respond with a warm 'Great idea babe, let's start planning.' He responds, nay, explodes into aforementioned panic. And then the idea of 'moving in' takes on a whole new meaning. It turns itself into a big fat ultimatum-inducing 'issue'. How can a suggestion so innocent become something so ugly?

Well, mainly because to him the suggestion isn't quite so innocent. This isn't your fault, it isn't even his fault. It's the fault of the culture you've both been born into and the socialising you've been susceptible to since birth. Just like marriage has always been targeted far more at the girls than the boys, moving in together has a whole different meaning for him than it does for you. You see plush furnishings, lazy Sundays and exquisite dinner parties. He sees infringement on his mess, the loss of his favourite chair (the one he got from the supermarket that has a hole for his beer) and domestic nagging on a scale he hasn't seen since he was fifteen. Moving in together is just another example of the type of commitment that he probably sees as scary and threatening.

And is it any surprise? Men have bachelor pads, shag palaces, playboy mansions (OK, so that's just Hugh Hefner, but you get the idea . . .). The image of being a young, virile man living on your own is pretty sexy. Did James Bond have a girlfriend shaving her legs in his penthouse suite, screaming at him to grab a pint of milk on his way back from solving an international murder mystery? No. Does George Clooney have to be in by eleven because 'er indoors won't speak to him for four days if he isn't? No. Will his 'Your place or mine?' t-shirt work as well if he has to change the lettering to 'Back to ours then . . . again?' No. The point is that men often fear this commitment because, well, it just never sounded very fun.

So how can you compete with years of social conditioning that tells you that commitment is a good thing and him that it should be avoided like the plague? When he hears 'joint tenancy' or 'shared mortgage' his immediate interpretation is that his lifestyle will be cramped and his freedom relinquished. So do you have to surrender to the fact that he will never be ready to talk wallpaper and soft furnishings? Are you facing a lifetime of love à la Woody Allen and Mia Farrow, in separate homes? Not necessarily. With a little repackaging you could sell the idea of moving in together to him in minutes. Before you know it you'll be commissioning that tasteful arty portrait of the two of you canoodling to go above the stairs. Or not. Whatever takes your fancy . . .

And one final word of warning. As always, you need to be honest with yourself. Sure, it may be that he's scared of commitment, but, as we've seen, he might just be scared of committing to you. And deep down you know what to do about that. You need to have a frank conversation. Because if he doesn't feel that you're the one he wants to play house with now, then that might not change. It's better to discover this and confront it sooner rather than later. Now, assuming he's just a little nervous . . .

Here's what to do about it

Well, to start with, if you want to change his perception of this type of commitment, you need to understand it. To change commitment as viewed by him, you need to view it like he does. The fact is that he sees moving in as having huge potential for loss. On his part. We've established the fact that the single life has always been sold far more successfully to the boys than it has been to us. So what is he scared of losing? Independence? His Friday nights with the boys? His favourite chair? Work out what it is he's scared of and then you can suss out a way of convincing him that moving in together doesn't necessarily have to be about loss.

To do this you need to be able to turn the situation around so that he views 'moving in' as a far less threatening concept. You need to be able to focus on what he could actually *gain* from taking the next step. So upon his initial panic don't let the argument degenerate into a mess of ultimatums and demands. By saying, 'live with me or lose me!', you only make the idea seem less and less appealing. Phrases which are also to be avoided include: 'I want us to live together so I can keep an eye on you, and then I'll trust you more', 'I want to know what it will be like to live with you before we get married' (before he's even thought about proposing) and 'Moving in with me will prove you're serious about me.' Put a positive spin on the idea. So suggest that it might be good for practical reasons – after all, it will avoid those early-morning dashes and boring car journeys every day. Financially, it often makes sense to maintain, heat and power one home rather than two. Then talk about the genuine emotional benefits of sharing your living space. It's good to know that there's always somebody there for you at the end of those rubbish days when the photocopier attacks your presentation notes, your boss calls you the wrong name and your mid-morning coffee lands on your lap rather than your desk. When you need a kiss or cuddle or something more, the answer is likely to be in the next room as opposed to the next town. After a raucous night on the town or a chatty, lively dinner party, you'll always have somebody to debrief with. Make sure you make the positives obvious. Make sure that he knows he really stands to gain more from this than he will lose.

QUICK TIPS

1. Remind him of the fine balance between debonair bachelor playboy and sad old man living on his own. That should scare him.
2. Resell cohabitation to him. It's about gain, not loss. For both of you.
3. If all else fails, casually refer to your addiction to walking around naked at home all day.

Q. Why does he have such a high tolerance for dirt?

Here's What's Happening and, Why

OK this one is for those of you who are already living with your man, but it's also really useful groundwork for anyone even considering cohabiting. But let's start by saying here that this question doesn't necessarily apply to every man. There are men who know how to fold clothes and lay them in a drawer neatly. There are men who appreciate that dirty, smelly plates do not complement the feng shui you practise in your living room. There are men who cannot tolerate spills, stains, mess and disorder. The problem is that these men are in a tiny little minority.

There are for several reasons for this. For a start, we have to go back to that old chestnut: evolution. You see, you really should have listened to all those mind-numbing ancient history lessons, because often the best way to work out why things are the way they are now is to look at the way they used to be.

Prehistoric man wasn't too concerned with a little bit

of mess. It's hard to panic over a bit of clutter and a small lack of hygiene when you're covered in the blood of the boar you've just slaughtered. After a long, hard hunt for tonight's à la carte selection, the words on ancient man's lips were *not*, 'I say chaps, we stormed through that settlement back there rather quickly. What's say we pop back and tidy up after ourselves?' Arising in the morning, ancient man did not make the bed, iron his smock and do a little dusting before heading out to defend his territory and stalk his dinner. The situation was rather different for prehistoric women. While the hunters were hunting, the women were gathering. And tidying. And organising. Keeping the hut clean was the woman's job, just by definition of her being a woman. The equal rights commission wasn't quite as hot on sexual equality in 2000 BC. If you were a man you did manly things, and if you were a woman you did, well, everything else.

Now exchange the club for a briefcase and the animal hide for a suit. Oh, and exchange the wild-animal-chasing day job for something a little less energetic. And you can see how easily ancient man translates into modern man. By nature, partly due to the legacy of his ancestors, modern man just isn't great at being tidy, clean and hygienic. The combination of this and the fact that, by nature, as a woman, you're probably rather good at it explains why you clash on issues of cleanliness.

Another gender difference that could explain the conflict on this one is the fact that women plan and analyse far more than man. So we get home from work. We take off our jacket and hang it in the cupboard, because we know that that way it will be uncreased and ready for when we next need it. We take off our shoes and stack them neatly on the shoe rack, because we don't want to trip over them later. We hang our keys on the key hook, because we know that if they're left anywhere else the result will only be a lot of shouting and swearing when we can't find them later. The man, on the other hand, will get in, throw his bag on the floor by the door, hurl his jacket on the sofa and head to the fridge with no thought on the impact this haphazard style will have on his life at a later point. We call it lazy, he calls it normal. Men live far more for the 'here and now' than women. So if he abandons a greasy, crusty oven tray, he doesn't think about how hard it will be to clean later, whereas we can't sleep until we know it is, at the very least, soaking in some warm water.

And if you look at your man's more immediate history, the way he was brought up can have a huge impact on the way he runs his life now. So let's say you've met his family. And after every meal, which *she* has, of course, cooked, his mother clears the plates, washes them up and stores them neatly, before slogging through the three bin bags of dirty clothes your boyfriend has brought with him (despite the fairly recent installation of a jazzy new washer-dryer in his own kitchen) and ironing every item. Yes, pants and socks too. This should give you a couple of clues to explain his competence at dealing with household chores as an adult. Just because our generation managed to narrowly escape the assumption that the women should be in front of the stove and the men should be in the office, doesn't mean that you won't still feel the ripples from the generations before you who did believe that. Part of the battle here is forcing your man to accept that you won't be his second mother.

Here's what to do about it

So how do you that? Well, initially, before you start to housetrain your man, you need to go back to the idea that men aren't mind readers. (Well, most of them. If you're reading this and you happen to be going out with David Blaine, then apologies, but at least it does mean he's got no excuse.) If the pile of dirty pants accumulating on the kitchen table is starting to make you feel a little nauseous, then tell him! He might just not see anything wrong with his little 'habits', particularly if he's lived on his own for a while. If he's always washed his football boots in the sink, then he won't stop unless you ask him to. If he's always prepared meat, veg, fish and dog food on the same chopping board, then he probably doesn't realise it's a one-way ticket to food poisoning (although you might have expected that last bout of sickness to drive the message home . . .).

Don't be subtle. You might think that raising an eyebrow and tutting every time he blatantly skips the 'washing your hands' part of going to the toilet is adequate. It isn't. Women are tuned to pick up on these discreet signals of disparagement. A tut, a sigh, a shake of the head, a roll of the eyes can convey a thousand words to a woman. But to a man? Completely lost. So be direct. Just say, 'I'd really appreciate it if we could keep dirty clothes off the table, because it's untidy and unhygienic.' Don't just move the clothes every time. Don't do his washing up every time, albeit in a huge strop. Don't pick up after him, because – at the risk at sounding like the exasperated mother of a five-year-old – he'll never learn.

You're not being unreasonable, you're not being strict

or rigid. You're just setting a few ground rules. You don't need to let this become a big 'issue'. You just need to tell him a little about some general standards you expect. Don't go on about it, because then you really will sound like a nagging mother and nobody wants to go back to a teenager-parent relationship. Just be honest and direct.

QUICK TIPS

1. Be careful you don't slip into 'mother mode'. It really isn't your job to pick up after him.
2. Learn to identify which things you really can't accept and which things you can be a little more lenient with.
3. Tape hours of those bacteria adverts with the magnified luminous creature, and play them on repeat in the bedroom. Shock tactics can be very helpful.

Q. We've just moved in together. Why do we fight about money?

Here's what's happening and why

You never could have seen this one coming. Back in those blissful days when he had his place and you had yours you tried to anticipate every possible source of cohabitational friction. Cleaning duties? You implemented a comprehensive yet flexible rota. OK, he keeps mocking it and wearing that stupid pinny when he's carrying out his chores, but at least they're getting done. Him staggering in, smelly and drunk from the pub? You've established a very simple procedure whereby on these select occasions (every Friday night, then) he sleeps on the sofa in a sleeping bag. Your six-hour phone marathons? You begrudgingly agreed to limit non-essential (well, that's what he thinks!) calls to your mobile. You thought you had domestic harmony nailed. Never in a month of Sundays did you see yourself screaming like a madwoman with a calculator in one hand and a clutch of bills in the other.

Neither did you imagine yourself creeping in from the shops and stashing your lovely new purchases under the bed to avoid the inevitable raised eyebrows. You remember a time, before he developed his eagle eye for your bank statements, when your second favourite thing, after shopping, was the fashion show you'd do for him in your new gear. Never did you anticipate topping off a delightful meal with an Irish coffee and a whispered row about who picked up the bill last time. Before you lived together, you just used to take turns. Now, however, you find yourself rowing about how your hair straighteners use more units of electricity than his razor charger so you should pay more.

Of course, forty years ago you wouldn't have encountered any of these problems. In the sixties, traditional gender roles thrived. The man earned and organised the money, while the woman cooked, cleaned and raised the children. Admittedly, the woman did take responsibility for spending a share of the money, but the arguments were minimised by the fact that there really was no discussion. The man's views on spending and saving reigned supreme.

Now, of course, times have changed. Women are likely to earn just as much as their partners, if not more. The emphasis is strongly on a woman's right and, indeed, her responsibility to provide for herself. And, quite rightly, if you're earning just as much as your man, then you have every right to make equal decisions about what happens to that money.

Money is central to the power structure within your relationship. If your boyfriend earns more than you and can contribute more to the joint expenses of living together, this can make you feel that he has more control over what you spend as a couple and the things you do together. Many of the arguments caused by money can be attributed to the associations of power, dominance and control that go hand in hand with how much you bring home.

Also, talking about money is something that many of us feel hugely uncomfortable with. A lot of families operate on the basis that money is a private affair and to talk about it openly is rather naff. It is not uncommon to have absolutely no idea how much either of your parents has ever earned. Because of this background it can be hard to have a frank discussion with your man about how much both of you will be bringing in and how you expect to spend your hard-earned cash. So, instead, you communicate through a combination of material gestures, tuts, arguments over bills, spats in restaurants and judgements on each other's outgoings.

Here's what to do about it

Firstly, you need to bite the bullet and have an honest, open discussion with your man about money. It might sound silly, considering this man is the love of your life, but you need to view it as a business meeting. The sooner you can have this discussion, the better. When you live together, whether you are sharing a mortgage or just the phone bill, there will be outgoings that you need to take joint responsibility for. Muddling along, taking each bill as it comes, is bound to cause arguments due to the golden rule of living with somebody else – that is, you never, *ever* think you use as much electricity/spend as much time on the phone/have as many baths etc., etc. as the person you live with. So right from the beginning, decide what you will do. Maybe he takes the electricity bill, you take the phone bill, maybe you just split all bills right down the middle? Find a system and stick to it.

Merging every single penny is rarely a good idea. It's far too tempting to monitor every beer/computer game/shirt he buys and bring it up at a later date. The best system is often to keep hold of the purse strings for your own cash, but set up a joint account that you both pay into. This account can be used for joint expenses, like bills, home improvements and socialising together. Then your own individual accounts are your own responsibilities. In real terms, what this means is that he can't go mad about you spending sixty-five pounds on new lipgloss or buying three pairs of identical boots (in different colours . . .). Likewise, if he wants to squander a week's wages on a flashy new exhaust for his car or a weekend away with the boys, then that's his choice and at least it won't affect your joint money. This system means that you both feel like you're contributing, but you don't lose your individuality. It also avoids insecurities about who earns the most, because you will both be contributing the same to things you need as a couple.

And one final tip: whatever you do try to avoid being petty. Arguments consisting of 'But that's my yoghurt', 'Yeah, well you ate my clearly-labelled sausage roll' are never, ever productive. So don't waste time on them. If one of you starts being petty, it can be easy to slip into a spiral of arguments over that extra sixty pence left to pay on the gas bill and the five-minute phone call he made to his mum's mobile. Try to keep focused on the important issues and establish a set up that works best for both of you.

QUICK TIPS

1. Get one joint account for shared expenses, and keep everything else separate.
2. Retain the spontaneity, don't tot up the totals of little gifts and romantic gestures.
3. If you really can't get it to work, the loft is always a great place to hide those shopping bags . . .

Q. My partner's been unfaithful. Is this the end of the relationship?

Here's what's happening and why

Learning that your partner has been unfaithful can be one of the toughest things you'll ever go through. We've talked a lot about learning how not to see the behaviour of our partner as an immediate reflection of our own worth. This is easier said than done when your partner chooses to be with somebody else, whether that choice constitutes a moment of madness, or weeks, months or years of deception. An infidelity can feel like an attack on your relationship, your security and your own sense of self-worth. There is no doubt that finding out your man has cheated is a fairly traumatic experience. But it doesn't necessarily have to be the end of your relationship.

Now, of course, immediately after the revelation you will be met with scores of friends, sisters, hairdressers and general 'well-wishers' who will advocate a zero-tolerance policy. 'If he's cheated,' they tell you, 'it's over. Move on girlfriend, get over him – he's a scumbag.' And so on and so on. And nobody would recommend staying with somebody who has hurt you if that somebody is likely to hurt you again. But sometimes affairs can actually improve relationships, because they force us to look at the relationship in an entirely new context and address problems that have been simmering underneath the surface for too long. Sure, infidelity is a dirty, painful word, but it doesn't always spell the end.

And what if you're the one who's cheated? That's a bit different, of course. Lots of the emotions are different: you might be feeling guilty rather than angry, full of remorse rather than betrayed. But a lot of this advice applies whichever way the affair came about.

One thing to remember is that affairs are nearly always symptoms of problems and rarely the initial cause of them. So if you or your partner cheats, it is likely that there has been trouble in paradise long before one of you succumbed to the charms of somebody else. This, of course, is no excuse, but it can help to place the affair in context. The idea that men just have sex because they can, and it means nothing to them other than sex, is really just a big fat cliché. Because men often feel uncomfortable talking about their feelings, physical actions such as sex or violence can act as outlets. So if a man is failing to perform at work his self-esteem might suffer. Sleeping with his secretary might be the ego boost that he needs, especially if he finds it hard to talk to his girlfriend about what's really going on. Perhaps your sex life has dwindled and your partner has begun to feel neglected, so he looks elsewhere for intimacy. Again, these reasons do not constitute valid excuses, but they do highlight the areas that need to be looked at if you decide to give the relationship another chance.

So the point is you might decide that, personally, you just can't get over the betrayal. And that's fine. It is absolutely your prerogative to move on and say goodbye to the relationship. Equally, if you feel that the relationship can recover, don't feel pressurised into ending things. Because, actually, a little hiccup can be what you need to truly appreciate and work with your partner. And if you're the one who cheated and now you're full of regrets, you really need to pay attention to this bit because it will help you understand how your man is feeling. Here are a few pointers to help you with this . . .

Here's what to do about it

As hard as it seems, you really have to stop focusing on the actual act of betrayal itself. Questions like 'Was she better than me?', 'Were her boobs bigger than mine?' and 'What colour were her eyes?' might seem appropriate at the time, but in the long run they won't help you. All they will do is focus your mind on comparisons between yourself and the 'other woman'. Consequently, you are far more likely to see the infidelity as the result of a personal fault, rather than a fault of the relationship. Keep your focus on the problems that actually led to the betrayal, rather than the individual involved. There are no right answers to questions like 'What was she like in bed?' Think about it. What answer would satisfy you? There isn't one, so don't waste time asking the question. If it were the worst or the best sexual experience of his life, it still has no bearing on the situation between the two of you, so try to focus on the things you *can* work with.

Know yourself. Know whether you will ever be able to move on from this episode. Of course, at first you have every right to feel raw and slightly bitter. But how long will this last for? Because, although a lot of healing is obviously necessary, your relationship cannot go anywhere if the infidelity remains the most important thing in your life forever and a day. After the initial screaming and shouting has stopped, you basically have the choice of two courses of action. If you don't think you can ever regain the trust you had in your partner, then you need to say goodbye. Or, if you decide to stay with that person, you need to put the situation firmly behind you. Because staying with your man and punishing him every day of his life for one mistake is simply not an option. It won't make either of you happy. Be angry, be hurt, be sad, but be honest with your partner so that you can work with him to get over this. Don't store the feelings you have now, only to unleash them every time he forgets to feed the cat or pay the phone bill or put the loo seat down. For the relationship to move forward, you both need to move forward as individuals. Don't let one moment of madness become a defining feature of your relationship. Because making your partner pay for the mistake over and over and over again isn't really moving on from it.

While dwelling on the infidelity really isn't the way forward, you do have a right to be clear about the behaviour you need from him to feel safe and secure again. It is fair, if your trust has been damaged, that you make a few requests to help put it back together again. Be reasonable. Don't say, 'You have to call me every hour on the hour', because while your disgraced partner might agree, it is an impossible task to maintain and it isn't the way to sustain a healthy, functional relationship. You don't really want to speak to him every hour, you just want to be able to trust him again. So tell him you need time. That might mean time with him, it might mean time to yourself. Tell him you need more reassurance of his feelings for you. Tell him that you want to work on the communication in your relationship, so that in the future any problems will be dealt with properly. As long as your demands are reasonable and you are both honest with yourselves and each other, there's no reason that you can't rebuild your relationship. And more than that, there's no reason you can't improve on the trust you had established before the betrayal.

QUICK TIPS

1. It's easy to blame 'the other woman'. Don't. It was him that made a commitment to you and then broke it. Not her.
2. Move on, with him or without him. Learn to leave the infidelity in the past.
3. Brute violence and mindless vandalism might feel good for about five minutes. Communication and honesty will work for a whole lot longer.

Q. My boyfriend is watching porn. What should I do?

Here's what's happening and why

And you thought he was watching football. All of those

nights when you've left him on the sofa and headed to bed with a cup of tea and this week's *Heat* magazine. Admittedly, you wondered why United would be playing at midnight, but then it's football and there are a lot of things you don't understand – like the offside rule and why they all have to spit on the ground so much. And then one day you find out that it's not so much men in shorts grappling with each other that he's become so engrossed in. Rather, it's bouncy, buxom blondes doing the grappling. And you're pretty sure they're not wearing shorts. Or anything else for that matter. It's hard to decide what you're more disturbed by – the grunting and groaning that is coming from your TV speakers or the look of guilty panic spreading across your boyfriend's face. Suddenly the sophisticated twenty-something you are proud to call your man has degenerated into a naughty sixteen-year-old who's just been caught with a dirty magazine. Apart from the fact that he's not a sexually-deprived teenager. He's a grown man. With a beautiful girlfriend. And a healthy sex life. So what the hell is going on?

Has your whole relationship been a charade? Are his really meaningful relationships with Mindi, Cindi and the other bimbos in the latest bonkbuster? Were you a complete fool for thinking he would find that delicate new slip from la Senza sexy, when clearly what really gets him going is grown women with ridiculous boob jobs dressed as school girls? When you're in bed together, is he secretly wishing you'd call him 'Superstud' and tie him up? Or whatever it is they do in those videos. And can your sex life ever return to normal now that you know about his dirty little secret?

Well, firstly, the good news (or bad news, depending on

which way you look at it) is that really his attraction to porn isn't unusual or weird or dirty. The fact is that most men like porn. Now, of course, some women do too. But the way our brains are structured means that porn is far more likely to appeal to him than to you. This is because men are aroused primarily by visual stimulus and whereas women are too, they also tend to take other things into consideration.

Internet pornographers have found women much harder to target than men, because they need far more to arouse them than just a reel of visual shots. For example, a woman will want to know what the relationship is between two lovers: if they are in love, or whether this is a one-off or a secret affair. Then, she can become aroused by sexual images – but she needs the background info too. Men will respond far quicker and with more vigour to purely visual stimuli, therefore porn is far easier to market to the male brain.

Men are also more likely to be aroused by violent, aggressive sex, because they have up to twenty times more testosterone in their bodies than women. This type of sex might not fit in with what you two enjoy as a couple, so pornography is a way for him to 'indulge' without threatening his relationship with you.

So porn doesn't necessarily represent a massive problem for you as a couple, but how do you deal with it if you feel uncomfortable about his, ahem, 'viewing habits'?

Here's what to do about it

The key here is to not be punitive. Porn might not be what you're into, but the statistics show that it's perfectly normal for him to enjoy watching it. Don't make him feel like he is a dirty little pervert, just because you feel uncomfortable with the situation. If you truly have a massive problem with porn in your house because you find it degrading or disgusting, then you will have to speak to your partner about this and explain your standpoint. You might find that this is a boundary or a rule that you really need to stick by. You might find that you can be a little more lenient. Equally, if pornography has become a major point of your boyfriend's life, to the exclusion of other important aspects, like time with you in the bedroom, then clearly this is a more serious problem. You need to get to the bottom of his reasons for indulging more in fantasy sex than in real-life intimacy. Either way, be calm and direct, and explain your objections.

If, however, your problem is not with the actual idea of pornography, but more with the fact that it happens to be your boyfriend watching it, then the issue should be easier to address. Perhaps you feel left out of your boyfriend's secret world, where nobody wears any clothes and everybody reaches a multiple orgasm – every time. Perhaps you see your sex life very much as something the two of you share, and the idea of him viewing these separate fantasies on the side makes you feel excluded? Then you need to explain this to him. It's likely that the reason he hasn't spoken to you about watching porn is because he assumed you would disapprove. He probably sees it as a 'boy thing'. But there's no reason that the two of you can't enjoy watching together. Trying new things, whether they work out or just have you in fits of giggles at the ridiculous plot-lines, will inevitable bring you closer, because you are opening up to each other and sharing new experiences. If you want to join in, then do it.

Perhaps your problem with porn has more to do with

your own insecurities. When you see him clearly enjoying watching women with massive boobs, tiny waists and minimal pubic hair, you assume that that is the kind of woman he wants you to be. Does he want you to shout and scream and dominate in the way they do? Is he really waiting for you to agree to, or even suggest, the fairly indecent acts you can see happening on screen? Probably not, no. Most men with a healthy appreciation of porn instinctively separate what they find sexy to watch and the kind of intimacy they want in real life. Porn is probably just a fantasy to him. It doesn't have any impact on how he wants his real sex life to be. For example, aggressive, violent porn is likely to be a release for the kind of sex he never wants to have with you. His attraction to and feelings for you are linked to more aspects than just your bedroom performance, so remember this, and remind yourself that watching the occasional porno will never surpass the connection he has with you.

The most important point here, whether you feel comfortable with joining him or not, is ensuring that you don't make porn something he has to apologise for. It isn't a dirty little secret, or a perverse habit. If you don't feel comfortable with him watching it when you're around, then tell him this, and ask him to keep his porn to himself. Maybe you need to make a little space for him to enjoy this time alone. But just make sure you don't allow it to impact on your own self-esteem or the relationship as a whole. If you feel like it is, then address this with him.

QUICK TIPS

1. Remember, him liking porn is not weird. It's perfectly normal.

2. Try watching it with him. You might enjoy it, you might find it ridiculous – either way, you won't feel so threatened by it.

3. Changing your name to 'Debbie Does', and donning thigh-high boots and a dominatrix mask, is not an appropriate solution. Especially not in the supermarket.

Q. Why has he become so withdrawn and moody?

Here's what's happening and why

Now, you're fairly sure that when you met him he could speak. There was definite verbal communication. In fact, yes, you definitely recall a number of witty, sparkling exchanges. If you remember correctly, his deep, husky voice and engaging conversation were definite plus points when you first met. So you're not 100 per cent sure when these wonderful qualities diminished into a monotone grunt. 'Hi darling, how are you? How has your day gone?' – *Grunt*. 'What do you fancy for dinner tonight?' – *Grunt*. 'Shall we go out and grab something?' – 'No'. Oh, yes, you'd forgotten, 'no' and 'nothing' are the two surviving words of his long-forgotten extended vocabulary. As in the standard answers to 'Do you want to talk?' and 'What's wrong?' Why has your lovely boyfriend turned into a stroppy teenager? He sulks, he broods, he slams doors and, worst of all, he just doesn't speak. Now, as a woman, you can understand the rest – the moods, the tantrums etc., etc. – but why won't he talk to you about it?

Well, he's not a woman. In case you hadn't noticed, that permanent feature of your bed, your sofa and your kitchen (when you're lucky) is definitely a male-shaped specimen.

So when you have a problem, you might want to slam a few doors, kick a few things around the living room and then pour your heart out to him about your cash crisis/the office bitch who's picking on you/L.K. Bennett not having your size in those pink kitten heels, because that's what comes naturally. You know for a fact that a problem shared is a problem halved and that it's good to talk, and a whole bunch of other clichés that basically mean that expressing your emotions is beneficial. And you don't need to tell your tale of woe just once. Oh no. Once you've told him, you'll definitely be on the phone to tell your sister or your mother, just before you invite your best mate round 'to chat'. To you, talking about your troubles makes sense. But that's precisely because you are a woman.

Generally speaking, weeping, wailing and waffling do not come quite so easily to men. Thousands of years may have passed, but when the chips are down modern man is still far more likely to simply retreat into his cave. And just think. No talking. No chatting. No sharing. Just a spot of thinking. Or brooding. You talk it over, he mulls it over. But this can easily be misinterpreted. So while he's just having a bit of 'alone time', you start concocting elaborate fantasies concerning what's really going on inside his head. Maybe his lack of communication is a sign that he can't be bothered to talk to you anymore because he's just gone off you. Maybe he's having an affair and he can't trust himself to speak in case he gives himself away. Maybe he's trying to figure out the best way to leave you.

Because women are such verbal creatures, when there is a lack of verbal communication, it can be quite unnerving. And thus begins what psychologists call the 'Nag-withdraw' cycle. You want to know what's wrong, so you ask him. He fails to give you a satisfactory answer, so you ask him again – albeit with slightly different phrasing. Again he refuses to open up, so you push more and more, driving him further and further into his cave. Simply put, the more you try to find out what's wrong, the less likely he is to tell you. The less he confides in you, the more you want to interrogate him.

So how can you get him to talk to you about his problems? After all, you know he's there for you if you ever have a problem, and you want him to feel that he can turn to you. How do you know when you should press to find out what's eating him, and how do you know when to leave him to it? And is it possible to hire a translator to decipher those grunts?

Here's what to do about it

This advice contradicts everything your instinct tells you, but you really should just leave him alone. Just leave him be. If his natural instinct is to brood and think his problems over, then don't try to crowbar him out of that. In a relationship it should be perfectly acceptable for someone to withdraw for a while. We don't necessarily want to dissect every thought and every emotion with our partner, and this is particularly true for men. By trying to talk about what's up, you're trying to get him to behave in the way you would, and that isn't necessarily the way he deals with problems. So let him use his own coping strategy. And if that means withdrawing for a while, then that's fine, leave him to it.

That doesn't mean you have to move out, stay with your mum for a few days and warn your friends, the postman and the milkman to stay away whilst he broods. Giving him space doesn't mean you can't talk to him at all. It just means you don't harass him about his problems. In fact, the best thing you can do is just let him know that you're there if he needs you, but you appreciate that he wants to work this out on his own. It will help you to feel like you are supporting your man, and he'll probably feel far more comfortable confiding in you if he hasn't been pressurised into it.

And don't punish him for withdrawing. If you decide that your reaction will be to become twice as moody as he is, then you'll hit a brick wall. Becoming stroppy and sulky won't encourage him to talk to you. Rather, he'll feel like he isn't entitled to deal with his problems in his own way, and you'll simply enter into a competition over who can scowl the most and sigh the hardest. If he's ever helped you through a problem, then this is the time for you to reciprocate, by giving him the space and support to think things through. Relationships will go through phases when everything's sweetness and light, and they will go through phases when things are a little harder and fun doesn't flow so easily. Just remember: patience is not only a virtue, it's a certified relationship saver.

QUICK TIPS

1. Leave him to it. Don't hassle him.
2. Offer your support and an ear, but don't force it.
3. Retreating into a mental 'cave' is fine, but if he tries to build an actual cave on the lawn, then get planning permission first.

Q. He says I'm smothering him and I feel like we're never close enough. How can we resolve this?

Here's what's happening and why

Romeo and Juliet never had this problem. When Romeo rolled up at Juliet's window she didn't say, 'Look darling, I love you, but I need my space. Please, stop all this showing up in the middle of the night already! . . . You're smothering me!' Likewise, Prince Charming never turned around to Cinderella and said, 'Look babe, I really wanted this ball to be about me and the boys, can't you hop back in your pumpkin and I'll catch you back at home later?' So what has happened to your love story, when you want more, more, more and he can't away run fast enough?

It's natural that sometimes in relationships life dictates that we have a lot of time together and that at other times you feel like passing strangers in the night. As you come home, he grabs his jacket and kisses you goodbye. As you walk out the door, he settles in for the night. So, you try to compensate with regular phone calls, romantic little gestures and vigils by his desk, watching him work. If he's going to go down the pub, you might as well join him and grab some half-quality time together. If he's going to the mechanic, you might as well go along for the ride. If he's having a lunch break, you might as well be there. Which, to you, makes sense, because you are making the most of any possible time you can spend together. It gives you time to catch up on the important things and the not so important things. Yet, still, you can't help but feel that you just aren't connecting enough any more. Your time together isn't enough: it feels rushed and incomplete. You love this man, and you love being with him. So as far as you're concerned, Luther Vandross was right: when it comes to time together there's 'never too much'.

Apart from, his latest bombshell has revealed that your man is a little less Luther-like in his thinking. Because Luther never mentioned anything about feeling 'smothered'. Smothered! How can he be feeling smothered? You barely see each other! In fact, this last week you've only seen each other that day you turned up at his office, the day you surprised him at football training and on Friday evening when you joined him and the boys at the pub. And you've only spoken to him about four times each day. And that's been when you've called him. In fact, the more you think about it, you've been making considerably more effort to create time for you as a couple than he has. How dare he complain about feeling 'smothered' when you still feel like he is a million miles away?

Two completely different perceptions of your relationship is a sure sign of trouble. When one of you feels smothered and one of you feels the complete opposite, issues of power and space come into play. This also demonstrates another throwback to social and evolutionary conditioning. Men are often taught that they need to be solitary, independent creatures. They are conditioned to think that they need lots of space to make decisions and basically be a man. Conversely, women are conditioned to feel that they need somebody close. This probably links back to a time when men *were* responsible for making big decisions and women were taught to just stick close and obey. Men were allowed their own time and space, whereas much of a woman's time was wrapped up in obeying the man. Women were seen to be dependent, practically and emotionally, so they needed somebody close. Sure, a few bras have been burnt and a few equality wars won, but the roles and stereotypes from years gone by can still have repercussions within a modern relationship.

And more than that, within the relationship it's important to remember that there are two individuals. And you will both have different ideas about what constitutes a comfort level of closeness for you. Perhaps he is somebody who needs to spend every waking hour with his girlfriend. But if he isn't, and you're trying to impose this upon him, there's likely to be conflict. This links back to boundaries and expectations. When we enter into a relationship, we usually have quite clear ideas about how we want that relationship to function – it's just that we don't always communicate those ideas to our partner. One person might feel like every snatched moment together is a blessing – even if it's only the half an hour before you fall asleep every night – while somebody else might well fail to see the point of five minutes here and there, and would rather wait to the weekend to spend some proper time together. People want and need different things from relationships, and finding your balance as a couple through effective communication is the solution here.

Here's what to do about it

If there is such a massive gulf between your perceptions of your relationship, you have a fair bit of work to do as a couple. What's important is finding a comfort level that you are both happy with. There's no point in him feeling content if you still feel like he is too distant. And vice versa. You need to look firstly at why you see things so differently. Maybe your smothering is a reaction against his withdrawal, and to encourage him to come to you more you just need to chill out a bit and give him the space he's screaming out for. Perhaps you feel like you aren't getting enough quality time with him, so you overcompensate by trying to spend hours on the phone to him or joining in with activities that he sees primarily as 'me time'. Maybe you just feel shut out because he places such high importance on his alone time, whereas you would rather make the sacrifice if it meant you could spend more time as a couple.

The way to confront this might be to sit down and have a frank discussion. Be clear and direct about how you feel and what you need, but be open to compromise and sensitive to his feelings too. This isn't just about meeting your relationship boundaries. It's about satisfying his too. Maybe you could agree to set aside Friday evenings and Saturday mornings, and agree that, whatever happens during the week, you will always spend that time together. That way you won't be suffocating him out of desperation and confusion over when you will see him next, because you will have an agreed time already planned.

This is one of those issues that you need to confront as soon as it comes up, because if you don't it will grow worse and worse. If you continue to pursue him, he will only withdraw further and you could well find yourself in a predicament that has travelled well past the time for cosy compromise. Act now, before you drive each other further away.

And learn to read each other. Getting closer in a relationship means learning how to work out how your partner is feeling and what he needs. We all know an elderly couple who can finish each other's sentences. It's because of the same sixth sense that tells you your partner is ready to leave a party. Or is in a bad mood. Learn to pick up the signs that mean 'Leave me alone for a while, I need my space', so that you can walk away, close the door and wait for him to come to you. If he seems to get increasingly touchy when you attempt to talk to him and cuddle him during the football, then accept that this is time he wants to spend alone, and that's fine (as long as he comes and gives you a hug and a cup of tea at half time . . .).

QUICK TIPS

1. Calm down. If you give him space, he's more likely to want to be closer.
2. Learn to read the signs that scream 'Go away!'
3. Surprise him by being unavailable to him every now and then – shift the balance.

Q. How do I tell him that I want to take this relationship all the way to the altar?

Here's what's happening and why

You just can't help it. You walk past a jewellers and you ignore the watches, the pretty necklaces, the dainty ear-rings. Because now, you're all about the rings. Dainty gold ones with whopping big stones at that. Or you walk into a newsagents and you know you're meant to be picking up *Heat* for your best mate at work, but you can't help but let your gaze wander to the beautiful forbidden sights that lie a little further up the shelves. You've found your favourite type of fantasy magazine. It's full of women . . . all wearing pristine white gowns, beautiful tiaras and shimmering veils. You've even noticed that the DVDs you keep watching on repeat cycle have a similar theme. You notice this as you concurrently wonder if watching *My Big Fat Greek Wedding*, *Father of the Bride* and *Muriel's Wedding*, six times each in one week is a productive use of your valuable time or, indeed, healthy. You can't help it. You can barely admit it. You've been sucked in. You want a wedding.

And more than that, you want to be *married*. And even more than that, you want to be married *to him*. It's not just about the fuss, the glamour, the excitement, the dress, the ring, the party (although admittedly, you're prepared to endure all of this in the name of true love . . .), you actually want to be his wife. Sure, you know he loves you, and you know you love him, and you trust each other, and you feel secure. You don't *need* to get married. It wouldn't make you feel more complete or more confident. But it would make you proud. You want to be able to sign his name not yours. You want to introduce him as your husband. You want to be an amazing wife. And you want to get him in a top hat and tails.

Apart from, there's one tiny hitch. Obviously, all the planning's in place. The venue is as good as booked. Your mother has found a brooch that perfectly matches her hat. And you're pretty sure they're still holding that dress for you at the bridal boutique. The tiny, tiny, miniscule hitch is that he hasn't asked you to, well, get hitched. Not a hint. Your diary is clear for the next eight months – no romantic trips with ample potential for the perfect proposal planned. You haven't found him sneakily examining your rings to establish your size. And when he was chatting on the phone the other night, you're pretty sure he described his recently-engaged friend as 'a mug'. Charming.

So what do you do when you really are ready to take the relationship up the aisle, and the idea doesn't appear to have crossed his mind? How many of those bridal magazines can you casually drape around the flat before he gets the hint? And if he doesn't get the hint, are you going to have to take matters into your own hands and get down on one knee next time you pop out for a slap-up meal?

Here's what to do about it

Well, this advice might well be a little late by now. But you really should be honest about marriage from the start. Now, that doesn't mean your conversation on your first date should consist of 'How's your starter? Oh, and how do you feel about marriage? Because if you're not up for it, we might as well call for the bill now.' Try it by all means, but you might find that the first date rapidly turns into your last. No, what I mean is that if, right from the start, he's been adamant that he sees the institution of marriage as a phoney waste of money, then don't nod your head enthusiastically and pretend you agree. 'God yeah, marriage schmarriage! Weddings are so yesterday. I'd rather die!'

It really might not seem like a particularly big porky to tell when sat in a restaurant on a first date, but an important thing to remember about telling lies on first dates is that they always come back to haunt you. So, when you say you're a part-time model, he will eventually find out that what you really mean is that you were Little Miss

Puddleton-on-Sea when you were eight. It means that he'll find out that 'I barely eat anything, I've got the appetite of a sparrow' actually means 'I wish you'd go to the toilet so I could scoff some of yours. I'm starving, I could eat a horse.' And it means that your man might just believe that you think the same way as him about marriage. If you've always played along with his 'marriage sucks' attitude, then you can hardly be surprised when, years down the line, he still hates marriage, and what's more, he thinks you do too.

So be honest right through your relationship. Letting him know you want to get married doesn't mean you have to propose to him on a regular basis, it just means you have to make subtle hints that let him know you're not completely opposed to the idea. So you could say, 'I do see myself getting married at some point,' or 'If you and I ever have kids, I really would like us to be married first.' These little hints mean that if he *is* dusting off his oldest suit and doing a little ring browsing himself, he knows that you are thinking about marriage too. Because perhaps your man *doesn't* have an allergic reaction to marriage. Maybe he just doesn't know how you feel about it. Sure, you might have been obsessing over that white dress and mulling over the pros and cons of a castle in the winter or a church in the springtime, but how does he know that? If you learn one thing from *The Man Manual*, learn this – men cannot mind read. They really can't. Bless them. So sometimes you have to help them out. If you think he's just waiting till he's sure he won't make a complete plonker of himself, then let him know that you're ready too.

And you know there is one option left. You could always pop the question yourself. Don't recoil in horror at the very suggestion. This, ladies, is the twenty-first century. We want equality when it comes to jobs, pay and opportunities, so why not when it comes to getting down on one knee? Thousands of couples propose simultaneously these days, and it can be a beautiful moment when a man and a woman just decide, with no planning or preparation, that one moment is the right one. Forget proposing on a tacky talk show, forget massive public declarations, forget skywriters, just be truthful and sincere. He'll probably be delighted you've taken matters into your own hands, well, onto your own ring finger.

QUICK TIPS

1. Men aren't stupid (regardless of the little jibes levelled at them by *The Man Manual*). Try not to make your wedding hints too brazen. Leaving a bridal gown on the coffee table is *too* much . . .
2. Be honest about your desire to marry him eventually.
3. If he will never be the marrying kind, then ask yourself if you are truly happy with that.

Q. I love him, but I just don't see us together forever. Should I end it?

Here's what's happening and why

You've never had so much fun in your life. Sometimes you laugh so hard you fear for your internal organs. You chuckle, you chortle, you guffaw and, much to your embarrassment, you occasionally snort. And he's devastatingly handsome. You feel the glares of jealous girls in the street and you love every minute. In fact, your standard reaction to the whispered exclamations of 'Wow! Look at him! He is so gorgeous!' is to firmly and territorially grab his bottom. He confirms every good thought you have about yourself and then some. If you think you look good, he thinks you look spectacular. If you think you've done something well, he thinks you've done brilliantly. He supports you, he looks after you, he lets you look after him and he's the sexiest creature you've ever laid eyes upon.

You can't help but rave about him to your friends, your family, your colleagues, your hairdresser – *ok* everyone. You know you sound smug and self-obsessed, but you're not particularly bothered. You've found somebody wonderful and you won't curb your enthusiasm just because the person you're talking to is having a little difficulty locating cloud nine. So, over a café latte and a pain au chocolate you find yourself detailing his wonderful ironing talent and doing a perfect impression of his cute 'just woken up' yawns. Your sister (who, if you're honest doesn't look overly impressed with your impersonations) stifles a yawn and says, 'So is he the one then? When are you going to get married?' And for the first time in twenty-six years she's found a way of shutting you up. You pause, shove a mouthful of pastry in and splutter 'Erryeah! Of course!'

Apart from, you're not sure, are you? If you're truly honest, for the first time in your life you're in a relationship that doesn't involve endless crystal gazing. You aren't picturing him in a frock suit, trembling with pride as you waltz up the aisle, resplendent in white. You don't sit around for hours, feigning deep thought when really you're dreaming up baby names that match his surname (and wishing Gwyneth and Chris hadn't nabbed 'Apple' first).

And you don't even know what his views on marriage are because, well, it just hasn't come up. You can't quite believe how many relationships you've been in where the future was planned down to the wedding cake. And they all bit the dust. Now, you're with somebody who is amazing and who makes you feel amazing. But you just don't think about the future with him, beyond what you'll make him for dinner tonight. (And even that's a bit hazy. Pasta in a sauce again?)

So, should you bin him and start auditioning for the co-star in your romantic drama? If you can't see yourself with him forever, then what's the point? Sure, it's a perfect relationship and he is an amazing boyfriend, but you want happily ever after and what if he really isn't it? If you can't see into the future with him, does it mean you're doomed to failure?

Here's what to do about it

This is the easiest action plan in *The Man Manual*. Because the 'what you do about it' is nothing. Absolutely nothing. Zero. Nada. Niente. Not imagining your current man as the Mr to your Mrs is not the end of the world, or your relationship, for that matter. So don't waste valuable time and energy stressing out about it. Some things are forever, some things aren't, and the only way you will know is once forever's been and gone. If things are pretty good at the moment, then live for the moment. It's a cliché, but life really is too short to obsess about tomorrow. Don't feel like you need to set out objectives and expectations for your relationship constantly, at every single stage, especially if you're only doing it so you can clarify things for other people. If your answer to 'where's your relationship going?' is 'Well, who knows?', it doesn't make your relationship a failure. You should be spontaneous. Not having an exact road map for where you are heading as a couple means that you are freer to enjoy some scenic detours, and find your way together.

The important thing to remember is that relationships serve different purposes. Not all of them are destined to last a lifetime. But some will help you learn the things you need to know to find happiness within that special bond with somebody else. One relationship might teach you about rejection or pain or fear. Another might teach you about yourself. Don't see relationships as the be all and end all. Use them as learning tools.

And things might change. You might not be searching for something old, something new just yet, but that doesn't mean that you will never see your man as marriage material. Just as people fall out of love, people can fall more deeply in love, and if everything seems happy and healthy now, then there's no reason why that can't happen for you. If it doesn't, then remember there's no such thing as wasted time when it comes to relationships.

QUICK TIPS

1. Live in the moment, not for the future.
2. Don't feel pressurised by everyone else to establish exactly where your relationship is heading.
3. Don't end it because he isn't the man of your dreams. Dreams change.

HAPPILY EVER AFTER –
IN THE REAL WORLD . . .

Snow White got her happily ever after. So did Cinderella. So does every woman in every single romantic comedy we go and see. They fall in love, they realise they're in love, they tell each other they're in love. And that's it. Cut. It's a wrap. Curtain Down. But think about it like this. Imagine if the tale of Cinderella and her Prince Charming had continued beyond the last page. What happened after the rather optimistic storyteller dictated a 'happily ever after'? What if the story continued, 'And they lived happily ever after. Until they got back to the castle when Cinderella found that the Prince had left his Indian takeaway in the lounge and his skanky football kit on the table. Then Cinderella was very cross and she called the prince a selfish b#*@!*! And then the Prince sulked for six days in the pub, with his court jesters.' Maybe Rapunzel and her prince had furious fights about him pulling her hair, shortly after their 'happily ever after'. Or perhaps just after the credits rolled in *Pretty Woman*, Richard Gere and Julia Roberts had a big row about her, ahem, past career choices. Maybe Romeo and Juliet lived to find that that vial of poison might have been a damn sight easier than dealing with her commitment issues and his smothering clinginess. I mean a girl needs her downtime – having her man appear on her balcony every five minutes is not conducive to effective beauty sleep.

The biggest lie we are sold about relationships is that they are easy. Films, fairytales and nursery rhymes tell us that happily ever after is the norm. Jack and Jill went up the hill to fetch a pail of water – nobody mentions the blazing row they had on the way about who was carrying the bucket.

The fact is that sometimes 'happily ever after' does exist – sometimes love is hearts and flowers – but sometimes it isn't. And real happiness means that you take the bad with the good. So sometimes you feel like you want to kill him, and other times you feel like you don't deserve him because he's so amazing. That is just the real nature of 'happily ever after'. Don't ever stop trying to make your relationship work, because there is always work to be done.

The Man Manual should have helped you understand a few of the differences between men and woman. We cry, they tend not to. We moan, they don't. We focus on the problem, they focus on the solution. We talk, they bottle. (To quote just a few examples.) Being raised as a man is very different to being raised as a woman, and this means that we react differently to different things. That's not a matter of opinion, it has been proved over and over again, study after study. Our brains have been analysed and our behaviour scrutinised for years, and some general observations can certainly be made. Now, of course, not every man conforms to the behaviour we've described throughout *The Man Manual*, but the advice given is based on thousands of letters that suggest that many of you are going out with a man who pretty much behaves in this way. If your man doesn't display fear of commitment or a fascination with porn or a worryingly high tolerance to grub and grime, then it appears that you should consider yourself very lucky indeed.

The point of highlighting these differences is not to emphasise the gulf in understanding that confuses many couples. The point is not to drive us further apart from men. What *The Man Manual* does is to help you understand a very simple fact. You are going out with a man, not another woman. So he might not understand your obsession with shoes, just like you don't understand his penchant for football stats. You might find his cave sulking infuriating, while he finds your incessant urge to talk, wildly irritating. And that's fine because we are meant to be different. *The Man Manual* should bring you closer together, because it should place a little background info behind his behaviour and show you the best way to interact with him.

Sometimes it can be hard to understand why, if men and women are supposed to mate and live happily ever after, we are so amazingly different. Surely if he thought just like you did and vice versa, relationships would be a walk in the park? They'd be a breeze. Wouldn't they? Well no. Because it is the differences we become so exasperated with that ensure our relationships have a fighting chance of working in the first place. Bonding with people who are different from us means we have every angle covered. So he might be your calming influence, while you inspire passion and enthusiasm within him. Or he might be painfully shy, and you are the one who brings him out of his shell in social situations. Your life might be a complete mess, from your bedroom to your desk, while he is obsessed with tidiness. Your relationship will work because of your differences, not in spite of them. If we always interacted with people who thought exactly the same way as we did, then we would never learn anything. In life, we need to experience different things to broaden our knowledge and grow as people. It's why you go to school, it's why people trek halfway around the world to the remotest, most obscure places. If you approach your relationships with the same thirst for knowledge as a quest for new horizons, then you will gain the most from them. Embrace the differences between you and your man, use them to learn about love, life and yourself. And use *The Man Manual* to guide you on your way to your own happily ever after . . .